Kermit & Shelly,
God's blessings to you!
Tom Hesson

D1508768

What's On God's Sin List for Today?

What's On God's Sin List for Today?

Tom Hobson

WIPF & STOCK · Eugene, Oregon

WHAT'S ON GOD'S SIN LIST FOR TODAY?

Wipf & Stock
An Imprint of Wipf and Stock Publishers
199 W. 8th Ave., Suite 3
Eugene, OR 97401
www.wipfandstock.com

ISBN 13: 978-1-61097-2796

Manufactured in the U.S.A.

This book is heavily indebted to the loving companionship of my wife of more than thirty-two years, Catherine. Her emotional support has been what makes this book her contribution to the world of scholarship as much as it is mine.

Contents

Abbreviations

ABL	Robert F. Harper, *Assyrian and Babylonian Letters*
ʿ*Abod. Zar.*	ʿ*Abodah Zarah*
ʾ*Abot R. Nat.*	ʾ*Abot de Rabbi Nathan*
ADD	Claude H. W. Johns, *Assyrian Deeds and Documents*
Agr.	Marcus Cato, *On Agriculture*
Am.	Ovid, *Amores*
Ant.	Flavius Josephus, *Antiquities of the Jews*
Apoc. Pet.	*Apocalypse of Peter*
Apol.	Tertullian, *Apology*
ARM	*Archives Royales de Mari* (series)
Autol.	Theophilus of Antioch, *To Autolycus*
B.Bat.	*Baba Batra*
B. Meṣiʿa	*Baba Meṣiʿa*
B. Qam.	*Baba Qamma*
Barn.	*Barnabas*
Ben.	Seneca, *On Benefits*
Ber.	*Berakot*
C. Ap.	Flavius Josephus, *Against Apion*
CH	Code of Hammurabi
Clu.	Cicero, *In Defense of Cluentius*
CTA	*Corpus des tablettes en cunéiformes alphabétiques*
Did.	*Didache*
Div.	Cicero, *De Divinatiore*

Eth. nic.	Aristotle, *Nicomachean Ethic*
Hell.	Xenophon, *History of Greece*
Ḥul.	*Ḥullin*
Hypoth.	Philo, *Hypothetica*
IDB	*Interpreter's Dictionary of the Bible*
Is.	*Os.* Plutarch, *Isis and Osiris*
Jul.	Suetonius, *Julius Caesar*
Kel.	*Kelim*
KJV	King James Version
Leg.	Athenagoras, *Embassy on Behalf of the Christians*
Let. Aris.	*Letter of Aristeas*
MAL	Middle Assyrian Laws
Mak.	*Makkot*
Mat. med.	Dioscorides, *Materia medica*
NARGD	John N. Postgate, *Neo-Assyrian Royal Grants and Decrees*
Nat.	Pliny, *Natural History*
Near.	Demosthenes, *Against Nearea*
Nic.	Isocrates, *Nicocles*
Nid.	*Niddah*
Od.	Homer, *Odyssey*
ʾ*Ohal.*	*Ohalot*
Paed.	Clement of Alexandria, *Christ the Educator*
Pol.	Aristotle, *Politics*
Prot.	Clement of Alexandria, *Exhortation to the Heathen*
Qidd.	*Qiddušin*
Resp.	Plato, *Republic*
RIMA	Royal Inscriptions of Mesopotamia Assyria (series)
Šabb.	*Šabbat*
Sacr.	Philo, *On the Sacrifices of Abel and Cain*

Sanh.	*Sanhedrin*
Sat.	Juvenal, *Satires*
Spec.	Philo, *On the Special Laws*
Spect.	Tertullian, *On Spectacles*
Synt.	Athanasius, *Syntagma doctrinae ad monachos*
Tu. san.	Plutarch, *Advice on the Good Life*
UT	Cyrus Gordon, *Ugaritic Textbook*
Vet. med.	Hippocrates, *Ancient Medicine*

1

Which Laws Are Still God's Word to Us?

I F YOU HAD TOLD me thirty-five years ago that I would be writing an entire book on God's list of sins, I would never have believed it. Why would I ever write a whole book about God's laws? Back then, I used to see God's law as a problem from which I was glad to be delivered by the good news of God's grace. Yes, I assumed that Christians are not free to openly flout God's law, but I resisted every voice I heard out there claiming that we needed to obey God's law if we were truly saved.

Yet today, our world has changed so much in the past thirty years that I find myself on the same side as those voices I used to oppose. In a world that believes that we are free to live however we please and make up our own rules, I find myself defending the truth that parts of God's law are still valid and binding on us today.

But which laws are we talking about? The question is an age-old question: Which parts of God's law are timeless and universal, and which laws were only intended for ancient Israel? The problem is that today, lots of people claim that there is no way to tell, that there are no clear answers to the question, "What has God said?"

When we hear people debate about ethics today, we often hear them lump commands from the Bible together indiscriminately. We hear them say, "The Torah forbids homosexual behavior, but it also forbids wearing mixed fabric, and eating leavened bread during Passover. It's all a hopeless jumble, useless as any reliable source of ethical guidance." Many are those who claim that the Bible teaches no consistent sexual ethic, but endorses polygamy, concubinage, prostitution, and even incest.

Or consider the words of Barack Obama during the 2008 primary campaign: "Which passages of scripture should guide our public policy? Should we go with Leviticus, which suggests slavery is OK and that eating shellfish is an abomination? Or we could go with Deuteronomy, which suggests stoning your child if he strays from the faith? Or should we just stick to the Sermon on the Mount?"[1] Obama went on to call Jesus' Sermon on the Mount "a passage that is so radical that it's doubtful that our Defense Department would survive its application." Again, the aim in such an argument is to portray the Bible to be wildly and hopelessly diverse, and then conclude that it is useless as a moral or ethical guide.

The Westminster Confession (6.102–4) identifies three kinds of law in the Old Testament: the moral law (found in the Ten Commandments), which remains binding on us all; the ceremonial law, which has been set aside by the New Testament; and the judicial law, which was only for Israel, except for its principles of equity. But telling these three categories apart in specific cases is not as easy as it might seem.

How do we sort through the laws given in the Old Testament and discern which laws are only for Israel, and which ones are still God's word to us today? And what about the moral teachings of the New Testament? How do we sort out the various mix of data given to us by the New Testament writers? Is some of that teaching culturally relative rather than timeless? And if so, how can we tell? Does the New Testament lead us to believe that all sins are equally dangerous? Or does it warn us that some sins put our souls at higher risk than others? How do we know when the New Testament is merely lifting us to a higher plane of morality, and when it intends to warn us against plunging over steep drop-offs?

I would argue that, despite a chorus of different voices in the Bible that sound different notes, there *is* a consistent biblical ethic. As we read the Old Testament law, we find a category of particularly serious offenses (as indicated by the penalties attached to them) that are reaffirmed as valid moral issues by the New Testament. As we read the New Testament, we find a number of sin lists where certain behaviors are consistently ruled out of bounds. And as to the question of whether a New Testament command may be culturally conditioned, we may presume that if our cultural situation is comparable to the world in which God spoke, God's word to us is the same as God's word was to them.

It is claimed that the Bible's ethical teaching is hopelessly contra-dictory. But are these contradictions fundamental, or only apparent? In his book *Theological Diversity and the Authority of the Old Testament*, John Goldingay identifies at least four possible forms of contradiction in

---

1. Mooney, "Evangelist accuses Obama," lines 14–25.

the Bible: formal, contextual, substantial, and fundamental.[2] All of the first three types of contradiction may coexist in one consistent biblical message. The first two types are only apparent contradictions. The third allows for contrasting positions that do not necessarily rule each other out. Only the fourth category (cases such as Yahweh versus Baal) cannot allow for two or more options to be simultaneously true.

This book will attempt to put together a consistent picture of what forms of behavior the Bible identifies as sin, using the lists of sins found in both Testaments, and the tools I have proposed for sorting out which commands are timeless and universal, and which ones are only intended for the original audience of Scripture. This book will not attempt to utilize biblical teachings or lists of virtues that only appear in their positive form. For instance, the Bible teaches us to be good stewards of creation in Genesis 1. While that teaching is important to God and to me, it is only presented in positive form, and therefore, in order to maintain the focus of this study on boundaries that God has set up for us, a discussion of this subject will not be included here. We will, however, examine a selection of behaviors that have often been condemned as sin by Christians, but which receive little or no attention on the lists of sins given by God in Scripture.

After examining the sin lists found in both Testaments, we will take a closer look at the debates about whether sex outside of marriage, substance abuse, abortion, and gambling should still be regarded as sin by Christians in the twenty-first century AD. We will also look at sins such as stealing, lying, and other sins on which there has been greater consensus, both ancient and modern, to see how the Bible's teaching compares to the way these ethical issues were handled by surrounding cultures during the biblical period. Ancient law codes, the writings of Greeks and Romans, and the teachings of the rabbis in the New Testament period will provide some perspective for us.[3]

---

2. Goldingay, *Diversity*, 15–25.

3. One key source I will use for the teachings of the rabbis will be a book called the Mishnah, an early commentary on the Law of Moses that collects the opinions of a large number of rabbis on a variety of subjects. The Mishnah was put together around 200 AD. The Mishnah forms the core of the encyclopedia-sized book we know as the Talmud, which was finished around 500 AD. Because the Talmud is much later than the Mishnah, and therefore contains a lot of tradition that is unreliable and does not go back to New Testament times, we will rely on the Mishnah as our chief source for the teachings of the rabbis, even though the Mishnah also contains many traditions that

Before we begin, let me make this as clear as I can. This book is not designed to identify a list of do's and don'ts to be obeyed as the means of earning our way to heaven. None of us can reach God through any program of do's and don'ts. None of us is good enough! Paul teaches that all who rely on their obedience to God's law as their hope of salvation are under a curse, because the Law itself says, "Cursed is everyone who does not observe and obey all the things written in the book of the Law" (Gal 3:10, where Paul quotes Deut 27:26).

No, the purpose of this study is to try to help readers get a clearer picture of what God has identified as sin, in an age where many of the parts of that picture are in dispute. One reason to do so is so that we can avoid the earthly heartache of sin. Just as we study the laws of human health to discover how to avoid sickness, we need to know the eternal laws that we need to avoid breaking if we wish to avoid the inevitable pain of breaking them, so that we may know the earthly blessing of a life lived in harmony with God's loving prescriptions for our good.

The other reason we need to know the law of God is (surprise!) that if we love God, we will want to know both what pleases God, and what breaks the heart of God. Think of the everyday scenario where boy meets girl, and the two fall passionately in love. Both boy and girl want desperately to know: What gives him or her joy? What turns him or her off? In the same way, we need to know what God loves and hates. With these goals in mind, let's get started in our study.

clearly date to after 70 AD. Citations from the Mishnah are identified by an *m.* followed by the name of the "book" within the Mishnah, and the chapter and verse number (example: *m. 'Abot* 2:2).

2

The Old Testament Sin Lists

IT'S EASY TO UNDERSTAND why many Christians get confused about exactly what to do with the Old Testament. Do we need to give up pork and shellfish (Lev 11:1–30)? Is it a sin to eat the drippings from roast beef (remember the command not to eat blood in Lev 17:10–14)? Is it a sin to eat roadkill (Lev 17:15–16)? Is cross-dressing a crime (Deut 22:5)? What about tattoos (Lev 19:28)? Is charging interest a sin (Deut 23:19)? Shouldn't we stay out of church if we've had sex or an emission of semen, or we're having a menstrual period (Lev 15:16–24)? Shouldn't we be offering sacrifices when we sin, such as in Leviticus 5:27–28? And if not, why not? Why do we celebrate Christmas (which is commanded nowhere), but not any of the Jewish holidays (which *are* commanded in Leviticus 23)? What in the world do we do with that unusual command not to boil a kid in its mother's milk (Exod 23:19b; 34:26b; Deut 14:21)? And if none of these commands is for Christians today, then why should we bother to tithe or to observe the Sabbath?

The Old Testament's teaching about what is sin may be found written in between the lines of its stories and its poetry, but the clearest place to find its teaching about sin is in its laws. Tamar's seduction of her father-in-law (Genesis 38) is never clearly labeled as sin. Proverbs 23:29–35 and 31:4–5 warn against the downside of drunkenness, but they never label drunkenness as sin. And Joseph enslaves the Egyptian people in exchange for food (Gen 47:13–25), but we are never told whether that was a righteous act or an evil one.

Yes, we can learn from the moral teaching that is written in between the lines of Old Testament history and poetry, and even from some of the explicit teaching of the prophets. But we need the explicit teaching of the Old Testament laws to spell out what is not clearly spelled out elsewhere. For instance, in its historical sections, the Old Testament tells us about cases of incest, prostitution, fornication, and concubinage that it never clearly labels as sin in the story itself, but the Law of Moses corrects the potential mistaken impression that the Old Testament actually endorses these behaviors.

The Old Testament gives us our authoritative collection of laws from Moses. Just as the Gospels contain the authentic teachings of Jesus passed down through multiple witnesses, so the Torah (the first five books of the Bible) contains the authentic laws given to Moses, even though those laws appear to have been preserved for us in independent traditions. Just as we find variation and overlap in the four Gospels, there is also variation and overlap between the so-called Holiness Code (Leviticus 17–26), the Book of the Covenant (Exodus 20–23), the so-called priestly laws (scattered through Exodus, Leviticus, and Numbers), and Deuteronomy, but all of these have been brought together into one legal code, probably no later than David, possibly much earlier. These law collections are not the inventions of later legislators, but are reliable witnesses of what God spoke to Moses.

The laws in the Torah may be categorized according to the penalties attached to them. Consider the case where the Bible critic wishes to claim that three Torah commands (forbidding homosexual behavior, wearing mixed fabric, and eating leavened bread during Passover) are all equally serious. The problem with this type of argument is that it confuses three types of laws, all of which carry different penalties. The first law carries a death penalty, the second law carries no explicit penalty, and the third law calls for the offender to be "cut off from his/her people." Such a wholesale mixture of texts is not the right way to handle the Torah's teaching, because their penalties clearly show that these offenses are all to be treated differently.

Legal scholar Edwin Good writes, "A society's values may be negatively attested in its punishments for the crimes it most detests. The more serious the punishment, the more the offense represents the negation of what the society holds most dear. On this logic, those crimes for which the offender is put to death represent the most blatant rejection of the common values."[1] If Good is correct, the death penalty signals the most serious offenses in the Torah's system of crimes and punishments.

---

1. Good, "Punishment," 947.

The Old Testament has a legal system where some offenses may be seen to be worse than others (sort of like our "felonies" and "misdemeanors"), although nowhere is this system clearly spelled out. The most serious classes of offenses in the Torah are cases where the offender is to be either executed, or "cut off from one's people" (which may or may not be the same penalty). By contrast, stealing is not a death penalty crime in the Torah, and may therefore be considered a "misdemeanor" by comparison. Unlike the case for other ancient Near Eastern law codes,[2] property crimes in the Torah (such as stealing) carry purely economic penalties: offenders are punished in the pocketbook.

A second group of lesser offenses in the Torah are those that call for physical punishment. Only one offense in the Torah calls for bodily mutilation (Deut 25:11–12), a threat which may not have been actually carried out.[3] Only one offense (Deut 22:13–19: false accusation against a virgin of Israel) appears to call for lashing. Deuteronomy 25:1–3 says that judges may sentence an offender to up to forty lashes; however, it does not say what crimes call for lashing. A third category of misdemeanors in the Torah simply calls for the offering of a sacrifice. False testimony in court is punished by the same penalty that the liar had intended to impose on his/her neighbor for the crime of which the neighbor was falsely accused (Deut 19:16–20), which may have been either a felony or a misdemeanor. Coveting is a pure thought crime, which is punished only where it leads to crimes that already have penalties assigned to them by the Torah. A fourth category of misdemeanors in the Torah consists of laws that appear to have been purely instructive and had no civil penalty for their disobedience, such as the law against keeping both a wild mother bird and her young (Deut 22:6–7), or laws about allowing

2. The famous law code of King Hammurabi of Babylon (around 1700 BC) prescribes death for theft in Laws 6–10 and 22, although it also includes economic penalties within the same statutes, which may be a later attempt to make punishment for theft less severe.

3. By contrast, King Hammurabi of Babylon employs the following forms of bodily mutilation: the cutting off of ears (§282), hands (§§195, 226), tongues (§192), and breasts (§194), and the plucking out of eyes (§193), as well as authorizing sixty stripes with an ox whip for slapping a social superior in the face (§202), and dragging a deadbeat land renter through a field behind cattle (§256). The Middle Assyrian Laws (1100 BC) also authorize the cutting off of noses (§§4, 5, 15), and pouring hot pitch on a prostitute's head (§40), while one Alalakh tablet (tablet #61, from Iraq, around 1500 BC) calls for molten lead to be poured into the mouth of the person who defaults on a major purchase.

the poor to eat of one's harvest (Deut 23:24–25; 24:19–22), not muzzling an ox while it is harvesting grain (Deut 25:4), or not charging interest (Deut 23:19). The kosher food laws (Lev 11:1–23, Deut 14:3–21) carry no explicit penalty; however, the forbidden animals are all classified as unclean, and therefore they endanger the person who eats them or touches their corpses, under laws that do carry explicit penalties.

One might find a third class of felonies in the Torah: offenses where it is stated that the offender shall die, apparently immediately, by the hand of God rather than by human hands. For instance, Aaron is warned that he must wear his high-priestly robe when he appears before the altar, or else he will die (Exod 28:35). A total of nineteen such warnings are found in the Torah.[4] However, it is better to see these cases as warnings of automatic consequences (akin to warnings not to touch high-voltage electricity or to look at the sun with the naked eye), rather than offenses that may be considered more severe than others.

The undoubted "Class A felonies" in the Torah are the death penalty crimes. Almost all of these can be traced to one of the first seven of the Ten Commandments. The Torah commands a death penalty for:

- *Idolatry:* Exodus 22:20; Leviticus 20:1–3; Deuteronomy 17:2–7 (see also 13:1–18). Ancient Israel is the only nation in the ancient Near East that makes the worship of foreign gods a capital crime.

- *Witchcraft:* Exodus 22:17; Leviticus 20:27. An extension of the first commandment. Hammurabi's law and the Hittite Laws (near Israel, from 1400 BC) also consider this a capital crime.

- *Blasphemy:* Leviticus 24:10–16. An application of the third commandment.

- *Breaking the Sabbath:* Exodus 31:14–15; Numbers 15:32–36.

---

4. Exod 28:35; 28:43 (entering the sanctuary out-of-uniform); 30:20 (failure to wash before entering the sanctuary—also 30:21); Lev 8:35 (must stay in tent seven days during ordination); 10:6, 7 (Aaron's family must not grieve or leave the sanctuary after the deaths of Nadab and Abihu); 10:9 (no alcohol when entering sanctuary); 15:31 (must prevent uncleanness in sanctuary); 16:2 (must not appear before the mercy seat without sacrifice); 16:13 (must cover the mercy seat with a cloud of incense); 22:9 (must not profane the sanctuary by entering it unclean); Num 4:15 (Kohathites must not touch holy things—also 4:19, 20); 17:10 (penalty for continued rebellion); 18:3 (Levites must not touch sanctuary utensils); 18:22 (Israelites must not approach the tent of meeting); 18:32 (must not profane holy gifts).

- *Cursing or striking one's parent(s):* extensions of the fifth commandment. Exodus 21:15, 17; Leviticus 20:9. Instead of death, Hammurabi calls for cutting off the hand of a child who strikes one's parent.

- *Juvenile incorrigibility:* Deuteronomy 21:18–21. Another extension of the fifth commandment.

- *Murder:* Genesis 9:5–6; Exodus 21:12–14; Leviticus 24:17, 21; Numbers 35:16–34; Deuteronomy 19:11–3.

- *Adultery:* Leviticus 20:10; Deuteronomy 22:22–24. This offense is included under the seventh commandment, together with all the offenses in the next four categories.

- *Fornication by a girl living in her father's house:* Deuteronomy 22:20–21 (see also Leviticus 21:9).

- *Intercourse with one's father's wife* (Leviticus 20:11), *daughter-in-law* (Leviticus 20:12), or *a wife and her mother* simultaneously (Leviticus 20:14).

- *Homosexual intercourse:* Leviticus 20:13.

- *Bestiality:* Exodus 22:19; Leviticus 20:15–16.

- *Kidnapping (stealing a person):* Exodus 21:16; Deuteronomy 24:7.

- *Causing the death of another person:* Exodus 21:23 ("life for life"); 21:29.

- *False testimony in court on a death penalty charge:* Deuteronomy 19:16–20.

- *Disobeying an official decision of a priest or judge:* Deuteronomy 17:8–13.

- *False prophecy:* Deuteronomy 18:20–22.

- *Trespass by a non-priest into the sanctuary:* Numbers 1:51, 3:10, 18:7.

It will be noted that sixteen of the twenty-one offenses listed above are directly related to one of the Ten Commandments, and two more (kidnapping, and liability in a fatal accident) are indirectly related. Furthermore, all but the last offense on the above list are matters that are reaffirmed as binding moral principles by the New Testament, although the New Testament does not command the death penalty for them. For instance, the New Testament does not explicitly mention incurable juvenile delinquency, but it does reaffirm "Honor your father and mother" as a binding moral principle.

It may also be noted that, while Israel is the only nation in its time and place to command the death penalty for idolatry, it does not follow the lead of other nations who command the death penalty for property crimes. Hammurabi, for example, prescribes death in numerous cases of stealing and white collar fraud, as well as for helping a slave escape (§15), failing to report criminal activity (§109), and for the cases of a nun entering a tavern (§110) and of a wayward wife who makes embarrassing unproved charges against her husband (§143).

A large number of other offenses in the Torah call for the offender to be "cut off from his/her people." They include:

- *Failure to be circumcised:* Genesis 17:14.

- *Eating leavened bread during Passover:* Exodus 12:15, 19.

- *Unauthorized production of sacred incense:* Exodus 30:33.

- *Unauthorized production of sacred anointing oil:* Exodus 30:38.

- *Profaning the Sabbath:* Exodus 31:14.

- *Eating sacrificial meat in a state of uncleanness:* Leviticus 7:20–21.

- *Eating blood:* Leviticus 7:27; 17:10; 17:14.

- *Eating sacrificial fat:* Leviticus 7:25.

- *Failing to slaughter meat as a sacrifice:* Leviticus 17:4, 9.

- *Committing "any of these abominations" listed in Leviticus 18* (according to v. 29), including various forms of incest, sacrifice to Molech, sex during menstruation, homosexual intercourse, and bestiality.

- *Eating sacrificial meat that has been left over until the third day:* Leviticus 19:8.

- *Offering children to Molech:* Leviticus 20:3–5.

- *Patronizing mediums and wizards:* Leviticus 20:6.

- *Brother-sister incest:* Leviticus 20:17.

- *Sex during menstruation:* Leviticus 20:18.

- *Approaching sacred gifts* that have been dedicated to YHWH, while one is in a state of uncleanness: Leviticus 22:3.

- *Failure to afflict oneself during Yom Kippur*: Leviticus 23:29.

- *Failure to keep the Passover* without a sufficient excuse: Numbers 9:13.

- *Sinning "with a high hand"*, that is, deliberately as opposed to unintentionally, "despising the word of YHWH": Numbers 15:30–31.

- *Failure to cleanse oneself with holy water* after defilement due to contact with a dead person: Numbers 19:13, 20.

What exactly is this penalty "cut off from one's people"? Both the ancient rabbis and the Greek translation of the Old Testament understood it to mean that God will destroy the offender. The Talmud (500 AD) predicted premature death in such cases (*b. Moʿed Qaṭ.* 28a). Donald Wold and Jacob Milgrom have reaffirmed the rabbinic view by arguing that the "cut off" penalty is a divine extermination curse involving no afterlife for the offender and no descendants.[5]

However, the first-century AD Jewish historian Josephus gives us evidence that the "cut off" penalty was actually expulsion from the community. Josephus writes that in Maccabean times (mid-second century BC), "And whenever anyone was accused by the people of Jerusalem of eating unclean food or violating the Sabbath or committing any other such sin, he would flee to the Shechemites, saying that he had been unjustly expelled" (*Ant.* 11.8.7). Also, while describing the Essenes (probably the people who produced the Dead Sea Scrolls), Josephus writes, "Men convicted of major offenses are expelled from the order, and the outcast often comes to a most miserable end; for bound as he is by oaths and customs he cannot share the diet of non-members, so is forced to eat grass till his starved body wastes away and he dies" (*War* 2.8.8). In the Dead Sea Scrolls, members are regularly expelled for offenses such as blasphemy and "sinning with a high hand" (Num 15:30–31, a "cut off" offense). Expelling the offender seems to be the way the Dead Sea Scrolls community carried out the penalty "cut off from one's people."[6]

---

5. Donald Wold, "Kareth;" Milgrom, *Leviticus*, 457–60.

6. For my summary of the evidence that "cut off from one's people" is expulsion from the Hebrew community, see appendix 1.

If "cut off from one's people" is a divine extermination curse rather than an expulsion penalty, then offenses such as eating leavened bread during Passover end up being punished more severely than murder, adultery, or Baal worship. The only cases in the Torah where "cut off" means "destruction" are laws where the death penalty is also declared, including Sabbath violation (Exod 31:14), Molech worship (Lev 20:1–5), and a few of the offenses from Leviticus 18 (covered by a blanket "cut off" penalty in Lev 18:29) for which a death penalty is specified in Leviticus 20. In those few cases where "cut off from one's people" is used with the death penalty, such as Exodus 31:14 and Leviticus 20:1 –5, it indicates an extreme form of removal. Otherwise, "cut off from one's people" appears to be a non-fatal form of removal from the Hebrew community.

If "cut off from one's people" is normally a less severe penalty than the death penalty, the implications of this conclusion are huge for Christian ethics. Laws that carry a death penalty appear to be timeless and universal, particularly in view of the fact that they are reaffirmed as valid moral issues for Christians by the New Testament. (Let us be clear, it is *not* the death penalty that is timeless and universal, it is the laws to which it is applied. The death penalty is a *signal* that a particular law is a Class A felony with God, as it were.) By contrast, laws where the penalty is expulsion appear to be laws that are only intended for Israel, and that are not reaffirmed by the New Testament as laws that are still binding on Christians today. So the requirement to circumcise, or the law against eating leaven during Passover, are punished by expulsion from the Hebrew community. These laws are only for Israel, while murder, adultery, and other capital crimes in the Torah are still binding moral issues for us today.

The Jews developed a belief that God only held the Gentile world responsible for obeying seven commands that God gave to Noah. God expected Gentiles to set up courts of justice, and to avoid idolatry, blasphemy, fornication, bloodshed, and stealing.[7] Any Gentile that obeyed these commands, God would judge to be righteous. The rest of the Law

---

7. *t. 'Abod. Zar.* 8:4. In the Talmud (b. *Sanh.* 56a), the commands are: establish law courts, and avoid blasphemy, idolatry, adultery, bloodshed, robbery, and eating flesh cut from a living animal. Other rabbis added consumption of blood from a living animal, and sorcery. See also *b. Yoma* 67b, which lists only idolatry, immorality, bloodshed, robbery, and blasphemy.

of Moses, including circumcision, the Sabbath, and the Jewish holidays, were only required for Israel.

Until he was circumcised, a Gentile was only obligated to keep the laws given to Noah. Once he was circumcised (or for a woman, once she was baptized), he was obligated to keep the whole Law that was given to Moses. That was precisely Paul's warning to the Galatians in Galatians 5:3. In Justin Martyr's *Dialogue With Trypho the Jew* (150 AD), Trypho cannot understand why the Christians refuse to be circumcised, which would give them protection (as Jews) from being killed by the Romans for refusing to worship Caesar. The answer why is because this act of conversion to Judaism involves a commitment to obey all the laws that God gave to Israel, including laws that are not intended for Gentiles who wish to follow the Jewish Messiah.

What do we do with the teachings we find in the Law of Moses that are not God's direct commands to us? Romans 15:4 says, "Whatever was written in former days was written for our instruction." The Old Covenant is not our contract with God, but yet it is foundational for our Christian faith. So as we read the Old Testament's laws on property crimes such as stealing, we see that God is more concerned with restitution than with punishment.[8] There is no capital punishment for any property crime other than for embezzlement of sacred loot from holy war, and the financial penalties for stealing are not sky-high, they are simply high enough to remove any incentive to steal. "Do not steal" is reaffirmed in the New Testament, yet it carries no death penalty in the Torah. The Torah's penalties for stealing are entirely in the pocketbook. We in twenty-first-century society usually throw the book at property crime, while we decriminalize most sexual immorality. The Torah, reaffirmed by the New Testament, does the reverse.

Likewise, the laws about ox-goring in Exodus 21:28–36 seem to have no relevance to us. Yet not only was the subject a major issue in other nearby ancient law codes, but these laws are also a model for dealing with modern liability issues. Substitute the words "If a pit bull attacks" for the words "If an ox gores," and we can instantly see how relevant these laws are to us today. Note that the beast is held criminally responsible for the taking of a human life, and its flesh is not allowed to be eaten, stressing the enormity of the crime, whereas in Babylonian law,

---

8. Greenberg, "Postulates," 18: "the leniency of biblical law in dealing with all types of property offenses is astonishing."

there is no penalty for the offending ox. Also, an owner whose willful failure to restrain a violent animal causes the death of a human being, receives the punishment for first-degree murder.

What does God want us to learn from Moses' laws on slavery in Exodus 21? First, we may notice that while the law code of King Hammurabi of Babylon (1700 BC) has its regulations on debt slavery at the end of the code, Moses puts them almost at the very beginning, which should not be surprising, since these are laws for a nation that has just been freed from slavery in Egypt. Second, we must note that the only kind of slavery that is sanctioned by these laws is debt slavery, which is not allowed for more than six years, except when a servant has his earlobe pierced in the presence of God to mark his permanent virtual adoption into his boss' family (Exod 21:5–6).

Compared to the surrounding nations of its day, Israel's laws on debt slavery were unprecedented in the humane treatment they required, perhaps because the Hebrews themselves had once been slaves in Egypt. It was forbidden to send escaped slaves back to their masters (Deut 23:15–16). Slaves were never set free elsewhere in the Near East merely because they had been injured by their masters, as they were in Israel (Exod 21:26–27). The Law of Moses punishes masters who beat their slaves to death (Exod 21:20). While Exodus 21:21 ("if the slave survives a day or two, he is not to be punished, for the slave is his money") is often read to mean that the slave is only a piece of property, the point may be that the economic loss to the master is punishment enough if the slave does not suffer immediate death (an indication that the master never intended to kill the slave in such a case). Similarly, the fact that thirty shekels of silver is paid to the owner of a slave who has been gored to death does not mean that the slave is less valuable than a free person; on the contrary, nobody gets any money if a free person is gored to death, except when the owner is subject to execution for criminal negligence, in which case an unlimited ransom for the life of the guilty party may be charged (Exod 21:30).

The laws about female debt slaves provide for the option of an unmarried female debt slave to become a permanent member of the family through marriage (Exod 21:7–11). While other Near Eastern laws also provide for such an arrangement, Shalom Paul points out that the Bible's laws differ from the cuneiform laws in the following ways:

(1) the girl is no longer considered a type of property that can be passed on from one husband to the next; (2) . . . if the purchaser refuses to marry her, he is guilty of a breach of contract and must let her be redeemed (vs. 8); (3) she must never be sold outside that one nuclear family (vs. 8); (4) if she is designated for her master's son, she is then treated like any other free maiden (vs. 9); (5) if the master should later take another wife, he must not fail to provide her (his first wife) with three basic necessities (vs. 10); (6) if he does not fulfill this responsibility, she is freed without having to make any payment (vs. 11).[9]

The formula "life for life, eye for eye, tooth for tooth, hand for hand, foot for foot, burn for burn, wound for wound, stripe for stripe" (Exod 21:23–24) is first given in the context of an accidental injury of a pregnant woman during a fight between men, a passage that will be discussed in the section on abortion in chapter 6. There is a parallel account of this law of retaliation in Leviticus 24:19–20, where it is also commanded that restitution be made in cases where an animal has been killed. There is some dispute about whether this so-called "law of retaliation" applies to accidents where there is no criminal liability. The case of accidental injury in a fight in Exodus 21:18–19 is helpful in applying this legal principle: if the injured party does not die, the one who caused the injury must pay for the victim's loss of time and for their complete recovery.

The "eye for an eye" law does not appear to have been applied literally except in cases of murder; such cases are usually compensated by Israel's ancient neighbors, and by Israel itself in later history, by monetary damage awards.[10] This law appears to function both to put a cap on damage awards, and to insure minimum compensation (rich and poor must pay the same). What is unique about Israelite law is that in cases of homicide, it prohibits both ransom (except the ox-goring case in Exod 21) and substitute liability; a child, for instance, cannot be executed for the sin of a parent (Deut 24:16). Numbers 35:31 declares, "You shall accept no ransom for the life of a murderer who is subject to the death penalty; a murderer must be put to death." Even cases of accidental homicide require that the guilty party remain in exile in a city of refuge until the

9. Paul, *Studies*, 53.

10. About five centuries before Moses, the Law of Eshnunna in Mesopotamia (Law 42) decreed that a severed nose should be compensated by sixty shekels of silver, and a tooth or an ear by thirty shekels of silver.

death of the high priest (Num 35:13–29). Note that Jesus teaches his followers to replace the "law of retaliation" with a policy of overcoming evil with good (Matt 5:38–42).

The commandments against eating carrion and against consumption of blood (Lev 17:10–16) are included in the advice given to Gentile converts by the Council of Jerusalem in Acts 15. But even though these commands are reaffirmed here in New Testament scripture by the earliest all-church council, we must ask whether these commands are given to us as timeless moral commands, or whether they are intended only for first-century Gentiles.

The Council's decision appears to be a compromise. It was designed to provide minimum standards by which Jewish believers could associate with Gentiles in the church. Instead of requiring total obedience to the Law of Moses, as the Pharisees would have required (Acts 15:1 tells us that some church members were Pharisees), the Council called for Gentiles to abstain merely from fornication, meat sacrificed to idols, carrion, and blood. All four of these would defile a person. However, only the first (and arguably the second) rose anywhere near the level of a capital crime. The last two never appear on any New Testament sin list (see next chapter), and are included by the Council because they are the two forms of ceremonial defilement that the church believed (under the guidance of the Holy Spirit) that Gentiles needed to avoid in order to honor the needs of Jewish followers of Jesus, as these Jewish Christians sought to both be faithful to the Torah and still associate with their Gentile brothers and sisters in faith.[11]

The kosher food laws are set aside by Jesus, according to Mark 7:19, "Thus he declared all foods clean." In fact, in the same chapter, Jesus declares that there is nothing external that can defile a person. Jesus says this in response to the complaint that his disciples are eating without ritually purifying their hands. Jesus is essentially setting aside the entire system of clean and unclean found in the Torah. So in cases such as ritual

---

11. The command against consuming blood carries a penalty of expulsion from the Jewish community, as we saw above. The eating of carrion also involves the consumption of blood, because the blood has not been properly drained. To eat such meat is an action that contaminates the eater in the same way that touching a corpse defiles a person. To avoid these two offenses, along with idolatry and fornication, constituted a bare minimum for Jewish Christians to expect from Gentiles. The Jerusalem Council prohibitions should also be read in light of the seven commands that the Jews believed that God gave to Noah (see above).

defilement by an emission of semen or a menstrual period, Christians are no longer bound by commands that were only intended for Israel.

Because Jesus has fulfilled the entire Law for us, and because his atonement was a once-and-for-all sacrifice for our sins (Heb 10:11–14), sacrifice is no longer necessary at those points where sacrifice is called for in the Mosaic law (Heb 10:18). These teachings remain the word of God to us, however, as we take note of the sins for which they are prescribed, and the details of how they are offered, details that point us to Christ as their fulfillment. Notice, however, that even Paul participates in sacrifice in Acts 21:16, where he fulfills a Nazirite vow (Num 6:1–21, especially verses 13–20) along with four other Jewish Christians.

What about the command "A woman shall not wear a man's apparel, nor shall a man put on a woman's garment; for whoever does such things is abhorrent to the Lord your God" (Deut 22:5)? This command is not reaffirmed in the New Testament, nor is there a death penalty (or any other penalty) assigned to this offense. However, this practice is said to be "abhorrent to the Lord" (*to ʿebath-YHWH*). What else in the Hebrew Bible is said to be "abhorrent to the Lord"? A search for this specific phrase finds the following list of offenses that turn God's stomach: idolatry (Deut 7:25, also 27:15), burning one's children in sacrifice (Deut 12:31, also 18:10), offering blemished sacrifices to God (Deut 17:1), witchcraft (seven kinds are listed in Deut 18:10–11), the wages of a female prostitute or of a male prostitute (literally "dog"—Deut 23:19), deceptive scales and measures (Deut 25:16, also Prov 20:10, 20:23), lying lips (Prov 12:22), sacrifice offered by the wicked (Prov 15:8), and an official who justifies the wicked or condemns the righteous (Prov 17:15). That's a pretty abhorrent list! To wear clothing that is clearly identified with the opposite gender is lumped in with idolatry, witchcraft, and fraud, all of which are reaffirmed as sin in the New Testament. The only ancient Near Eastern scholar who has researched this subject is Hoffner, who theorizes from the evidence that the use of opposite-sex clothing was a form of black magic intended to undermine the masculinity or femininity of one's enemy.[12]

True, much of this discussion hinges on the question of how to define men's and women's clothing. When Dr. J. Vernon McGee was asked on his radio program "Through the Bible Radio" what he thought about women wearing slacks, Dr. McGee said, "I've seen those things they call

12. Hoffner, Jr., "Symbols," 326–34.

women's slacks, and I wouldn't be caught dead in them!" It is true that in our culture, there are numerous kinds of clothes that are worn by both genders. This passage appears to point to the long-term intent to identify with the opposite gender, which finds its most extreme expression in surgical changes to one's gender (see chapter 7).

What about tattoos? Leviticus 19:28 says, "You shall not make any gashes in your flesh for the dead or tattoo any marks upon you." Again, this command is neither reaffirmed in the New Testament (or by any other ancient Near Eastern source), nor is there a death penalty assigned to it. It is surrounded by commands against witchcraft and sacred prostitution (Lev 19:26–31). But this command appears to be addressing a specific pagan practice that does not exist in today's world and is therefore not a command against tattoos that have no pagan message or symbolism. (It has been observed that in Revelation 19:16, Jesus has a name inscribed on his thigh when he returns: "King of kings and Lord of lords.")

What about the wearing of mixed fabric (Lev 19:19, Deut 22:11)? Because this command carries neither a death penalty nor any other explicit penalty, and because it is never reaffirmed in the New Testament, it is clearly a command only for Israel. But what was the purpose of this command? The term "mixed fabric" (šaʿaṭnez) appears to have been borrowed from Egyptian. It is a term used only in these two verses. Is this mixture of wool and linen evil or idolatrous? No, it appears that in this case, "mixtures belong to the sacred sphere."[13] The curtains for the Tabernacle (Exod 26:1,31) are made of fine twisted linen and colored yarn (although the word "yarn" is not in the text, it is implied). The same materials are used for the high priest's ephod (Exod 28:6; 39:29) and breastplate (Exod 28:15). The upshot of this command was that non-priests were forbidden to wear a material that was intended only for the holy place, just as they were forbidden to duplicate the incense and anointing oil used in the sanctuary (Exod 30:22–38).

What about the charging of interest? This practice is forbidden three times in the Law of Moses: Exodus 21:25, Leviticus 25:36–37, and Deuteronomy 23:19–20. In the first two passages, it is clear that survival loans to poor fellow Israelites are what is in view, not commercial loans. The purpose is so that one does not make profit off the poverty or misfortune of a fellow Israelite. Loans still must be repaid, on penalty of

---

13. Milgrom, *Leviticus* 3A, 1660. The Jewish historian Josephus agrees in *Ant.* 4.208.

forfeiting one's collateral, or even debt enslavement, but neither interest nor profit based on rising market prices may be earned from an impoverished fellow Israelite on a personal loan.[14] Christians today are not forbidden to make money through interest; indeed, even Israelites were allowed to make such loans to foreigners, as the Deuteronomy passage explicitly permits.

What about practices such as tithing, or the observance of the Sabbath or the Jewish holidays? The New Testament does not command tithing per se, but it does endorse the need for generous giving, and the Old Testament gives us the only evidence we have of what God recommends as a generous amount. And Jesus puts his endorsement on the tithe when he says that the Pharisees "tithe mint and dill and cumin" while neglecting justice, mercy, and faith, but then says, "These things you ought to have done, *without neglecting the others*" (Matt 23:23). Jesus wants to see his followers practice both: committed giving, and lifestyles of justice, mercy, and faith.

Jesus relaxes the strictness of many of his fellow Jews toward the Sabbath, and Paul almost sets it aside in Romans 14:5 where he says, "One person judges one day to be better than another, while another person judges all days to be alike. Let everyone be firmly convinced in their own mind." Likewise, in Colossians 2:16, Paul writes, "Therefore do not let anyone condemn you in matters of food and drink or of observing festivals, new moons, or sabbaths." We are free to observe, or not observe, the Jewish holidays, which still remain God's word to us in visible form. The Passover, Pentecost, and the Feast of Tabernacles ("Shelters" or "Shacks") all form part of our heritage as those who have been "grafted into" the people of the God of Israel. But because it is one of God's ten commands to the crowd at Mount Sinai, and especially because it carries a death penalty (which indicates its seriousness), the command to "Remember the seventh day, to keep it holy" (Exod 20:8) seems to call for a day to be kept holy by followers of Christ. The early church thought so, because they began to worship the God of Israel on Sundays, in celebration of the day Jesus rose from the dead. The Sabbath is not a direct explicit command to us, but it is one way we both express

14. According to the Mishnah, "No bargain may be made over manure unless it is already on the dungheap." (*m. B. Meṣi'a* 5:7) "Hillel used to say: A woman may not lend a loaf of bread to her neighbour unless she determines its value in money, lest wheat should rise in price and they be found partakers in usury." (*m. B. Meṣi'a* 5:9)

our devotion to God, and experience the benefits for which God gave this command to Israel.

A final question to be explained is what the Law of Moses means by "boiling a kid in its mother's milk." This prohibition is found repeated three times: in Exodus 23:19b, Exodus 34:26b, and Deuteronomy 14:21d, probably indicating that it was handed down from Moses by three independent sources. The tradition of the rabbis from Jesus' day onward is that this command means that God's people must avoid mixing milk and meat in their meals.[15] Even today, orthodox Judaism forbids cheeseburgers and pizza with meat, based on this legal interpretation; some even maintain separate sets of dishes for meat and dairy meals. However, on the basis of a Canaanite text (CTA 23:14 = UT 52:14), "Cook a kid in milk, a lamb in butter," current scholarship holds that this command is a prohibition of a Canaanite fertility ritual, a fact totally forgotten by later interpreters. Here we have an example of a law that was extremely relevant to Late Bronze Age Hebrews, but which was so specific that we have no equivalent to which it applies today.

As we examine the Old Testament sin lists found in the Law of Moses, the prohibitions we find there must each be examined individually, but they are not a hopeless, useless jumble. Based on criteria such as the presence of a death penalty, and whether or not a command is reaffirmed as a moral principle for Christians in the New Testament, we can make fairly clear distinctions between commands that are timeless and universal, and commands that are only intended for the Hebrew people. We turn now to the New Testament, to see what picture is presented to us in the sin lists we find there.

---

15. "No flesh may be cooked in milk excepting the flesh of fish and locusts, and no flesh may be served up together with cheese excepting the flesh of fish and locusts . . . A fowl may be served up on the table together with cheese, but it may not be eaten with it." (*m. Ḥul.* 8:1)

3

The New Testament Sin Lists

I CAN STILL REMEMBER the scene where the Taliban aimed their anti-aircraft guns (along with a rocket launcher and dynamite) to destroy two huge statues of Buddha carved into a mountainside in Afghanistan in 2001. Part of me reacted against the apparently needless destruction of some priceless works of art that were in no danger of being worshipped and that were no threat to anybody's faith. But part of me grudgingly admired the Taliban for having the guts to do what God commanded the people of Israel to do in Deuteronomy: destroy all pagan objects of worship in their land.

So what we do with an ancient book full of teachings, some of which are obviously intended for us to obey today, and some of which are obviously not? Should we establish cities of refuge for folks who have accidentally killed someone in an auto accident? Should we reinstitute the practice of debt slavery? Or what about the command to destroy all pagan objects of worship around us? (We must note that even the rabbis of Jesus' day, while they had plenty of rules as to how to avoid involvement in idolatry, never dared to destroy the Greek and Roman idols in their land.)

For Christians, Jesus is our authoritative interpreter of God's word to us in the Old Testament. Unlike the Quran, which has no authoritative word to set aside its violent teachings, Jesus is the one who sets aside God's command to wipe out the Canaanites with his teaching of love for enemies. His unspoken message to us is, "Don't try this at home."

As our authoritative interpreter of the Law of Moses, Jesus sets aside both the whole system of clean and unclean that God gave to Moses, and the kosher food laws, in Mark 7. Those are two humongous moves for Jesus to make as a teacher of God's law. These are major trademarks of Judaism. Now that he has done so, the question arises, If Jesus the rabbi can set aside the cleanliness laws and the kosher food laws, what else is up for grabs? Where do we draw the line? How much of the Law of Moses is still God's word for us today?

That's why Jesus gives us a sin list in Mark 7:21–23. As soon as he gets done telling us what does not defile the human person, Jesus gives us a partial list of what does defile the human person. Jesus gives some prominent examples of sins that are still on God's sin list for us today. A shorter version of this list can also be found in Matthew 15:18–20. It appears that Mark's version comes first, then Matthew edits the list for a more Jewish audience. While some may question whether Jesus actually spoke these words, or whether this list was simply invented by the early church for instructing new disciples, there is no reason not to believe that this list actually goes back to Jesus. Any rabbi like Jesus would have a *halakah* or code of conduct that he would teach to his followers.

Sin lists can be found, not only in the Bible, but elsewhere in Judaism, such as *Testament of Reuben* 3:2 and 1QS 4:9–11 in the Dead Sea Scrolls. In one passage, the Jewish philosopher Philo has a list of 146 vices (*Sacr.* 32).

A quick search through the New Testament yields a number of major passages where sins are itemized, passages which give us an apostolic consensus on what is sin. Raymond Collins finds a total of 110 sins in twenty-two lists he identifies in the New Testament.[1] By eliminating duplications, closely related terms, and vague terms such as "evil" or "wrongdoing," one may reduce this list to sixty-five sins and vices.

A closer look at these New Testament sin lists can help us in our current debate about sin. On these lists, we find echoes of many of the sins found on the two parallel versions of Jesus' list of sins that come from the heart that defile a person (Matt 15:18–20; Mark 7:20–23): fornication, adultery, murder, *blasphemia* (either blasphemy against God, or slander of fellow humans), and stealing. Where Matthew has "false witness" (specific breaking of the ninth commandment), Mark has *dolos*, "deceit," a broad term for all kinds of lying and deception. Unlike Matthew, Mark also includes greed and *aselgeia* on his list. The latter term refers to extreme forms of sexual immorality. This term may be Jesus' solitary veiled reference to homosexual behavior (see chapter 4 and appendix 2).

---

1. Collins, *Ethics*, 74–76.

Another example of a sin list is Paul's portrait of Gentile decadence in Romans 1:28–30. Romans 1 seems to be a sweeping indictment that aims at convicting the entire human race of sin that deserves judgment. Thrown into the mix are quite a few thought crimes and character qualities that are hard to measure or define, such as "evil" or "badness." After Paul's famous reference to both lesbian and male homosexual behavior in verses 26–27, Paul launches into a list that includes greed, envy, murder, strife, malice (*kakoētheia*), gossip, slander, hatred of God, insolence, pride, boastfulness, invention of evil, disobedience to parents, senselessness, untrustworthiness, lack of family affection (*astorgoi*, a term that includes willingness to kill unborn children or infants), and mercilessness.

Also, at the end of Romans 13 is a short list with sins that do not appear in chapter 1 (except *eris*, "strife"), but which do appear on other sin lists: *kōmoi* ("carousings"), drunkenness, *koitai* (slang for sexual encounters—surprisingly, *porneia* or "fornication" is not used anywhere in Romans), *aselgeiai* (extreme forms of sexual immorality), strife, and jealousy.

Paul warns the Corinthians not to associate with believers who are in serious sin, of which he gives a short list of examples (1 Cor 5:11). In his next chapter, he gives a similar but longer list of persons whom he says "shall not inherit the reign of God" (1 Cor 6:9–11) if they continue in their behavior. This warning gives this list particular importance: these sins are among those that Paul rates most serious. Included on his list here are fornication, idolatry, adultery, passive and active partners in homosexual intercourse (see chapter 4), stealing, greed, drunkenness, and reviling. Also, in 2 Corinthians 12:20–21, Paul says he fears that when he returns to Corinth, he will find strife, jealousy, anger, selfish ambition, slander, gossip, conceit, and disorder, and that he may have to mourn after those who have not repented of all the "uncleanness" (see chapter 4), fornication, and extreme sexual immorality they have practiced.

In Paul's catalogue of "deeds of the flesh" in Galatians 5:18–21, like in 1 Corinthians 6:9–11, we are reminded that "those who keep on living this way shall not inherit the reign of God," making this list another particularly important source as we assemble God's sin list. Paul identifies fornication, uncleanness, extreme sexual immorality, idolatry, witchcraft (*pharmakeia*—see chapter 5), enmity, strife, jealousy, anger, selfish ambition, dissension, "heresies," envy, drunkenness, and carousing on his sin list, which he concludes with the note that this is only a partial list. Surprisingly, murder is not on this list. This list in Galatians 5 becomes the most quoted list of sins in the writings of the early church.

In Ephesians and Colossians, Paul names a number of deeds "because of which the wrath of God is coming" (Col 3:6). After calling on his readers in Ephesians 4:17 to no longer live like the Gentiles do in extreme sexual immorality (*aselgeia*), Paul urges them in verse 31 to put away all bitterness, anger, wrath, screaming, *blasphemia*, and malice (*kakia*). In Ephesians 5:3–5, Paul insists that fornication and all impurity and greed "must not even be named among you," in other words, they must not even be spoken of as a Christian form of behavior. (In verse 12, he says it is "shameful even to speak of the things they do in secret.") Paul also rules out indecency, foolish talk, and "coarse jesting" (*eutrapelia*, a word used only here in the Bible). Using language that echoes the lists in 1 Corinthians and Galatians, Paul also warns the Ephesians that no fornicator, impure person (*akathartos*), or greedy person has an inheritance in the reign of God (Eph 5:5). In his letter to Ephesus, Paul also teaches believers to "put off falsehood" (4:25), "let the thief no longer steal" (4:28), and that no "rotten" (*sapros*) word should proceed from their mouths (4:29).

Paul uses similar language in his letter to the Colossians. He tells his readers to put to death in their bodily parts fornication, uncleanness, passion (*pathos*), "evil desire," and greed, and to put away wrath, anger, malice, *blasphemia*, and indecent language, followed by an exhortation not to lie to one another.

Paul's list of those for whom the Law is written in 1 Timothy 1 parallels the Ten Commandments. His first four descriptive terms (rebellious, ungodly, unholy, profane) describe a person who rejects their duty to God, which is the subject of the first four commandments. "Murderers of fathers and murderers of mothers" are extreme violations of the fifth commandment, while the generic "manslaughterers" covers the sixth. Fornicators and homosexuals (same word as 1 Cor 6:9, the only other time this word is used in the Bible) are both covered in the seventh commandment, while kidnappers are the only example of stealing that is given on this list. Liars and perjurers represent the ninth commandment, but there is no example of coveting on this list; it leaves off with "and whatever is contrary to sound doctrine."

Paul's checklists of leadership standards in 1 Timothy 3:2–7 and Titus 1:6–9 present us mostly with exemplary qualities to strive for rather than moral felonies. Both lists teach that a leader should not be a "striker" or quarrelsome, not a lover of money, and not *paroinos*, "given to much wine." Titus adds that a leader should not be *authadē* (too stubborn to be teachable) or quick-tempered. Failure to be hospitable need not disqualify one from office, but we might draw the line at drug or spouse abuse.

Paul's detailed description in 2 Timothy 3 of what human depravity will be like in the last days is much like his description of human depravity in Romans 1. Sins that appear elsewhere are: boasters, those who are haughty, slanderers (*blasphemoi*—the synonym *diaboloi* is also on this list), those who disobey parents, and those who lack family affection (*astorgoi*, also in Rom 1). The rest of Paul's list is more descriptive than it is a list of sins; he speaks of an age when people will be lovers of self, lovers of money, lovers of pleasure, ungrateful, haters of good, irreverent, implacable, savage, without self-control, treacherous, reckless, and conceited.

There are several short sin lists in 1 Peter. In 2:1, Peter tells his readers to put away all "malice" (*kakia*), deceit, "hypocrisies," envy and slander. In 4:3, he urges them to let the time that is past be enough for living like the Gentiles, in extreme sexual immorality, lust, drunkenness (*oinophlygia*, "inflamed with wine," a word only used here in the Bible), carousing, drinking, and lawless idolatry. And in 4:15, Peter says, Don't let any of you suffer as a murderer or a thief or an "evildoer" (unspecified), or a "meddler."

Finally, there is the double list of people who are excluded from the Holy City in Revelation 21:8 and 22:15. Included on both lists are witchcraft practitioners, fornicators, murderers, idol worshippers, and those who love and make lies. The first list includes the cowardly, the faithless, and "those who have been made abominable." The second list includes "dogs," a probable reference to those who practice homosexual behavior. The terms murder, witchcraft, fornication, theft, and idolatry are also named at the end of chapter 9 as sins from which people refused to repent after the plagues of that chapter.

Upon examination, some recurrent patterns emerge:

Matt 15	Mark 7	1 Cor 6	Gal 5	1 Tim 1	Rev 21–22
Phonoi	*Phonoi*			*Androphonoi*	*Phonoi*
Moicheiai	*Moicheia*	*Moichoi*			
Porneiai	*Porneiai*	*Pornoi*	*Porneia*	*Pornoi*	*Pornoi*
Klopai	*Klopai*	*Kleptai*			*Kleptai* (9:21)
	Pleonexia	*Pleonektai*			
		Eidololatria	*Eidololatria*		*Eidololatrai*
	Aselgeia	*Arsenokoitai*	*Aselgeia*	*Arsenokoitai*	*Kynes* (Deut 23:18)
			Pharmakeia		*Pharmakoi*
	Methusoi		*Methai*		

Note what is not on these lists. Sabbath-breaking, for instance, although it carries an Old Testament death penalty, is nowhere to be found on these lists of potentially deadly sins. Neither is one of today's moral felonies, domestic violence, which is condemned only on Paul's lists of qualifications for leadership in 1 Timothy 3:3 and Titus 1:7. (One could also argue that domestic violence is an extension of *phonos*, murder.) Meanwhile, theft and greed, which are not punishable by death in the Mosaic law, do appear on these lists of serious moral offenses.

One critical issue for interpretation is what Paul means by the term "inherit the reign of God." To say that certain sins endanger one's salvation seems to contradict Paul's theology of salvation by grace. One can only guess at what Paul means here, but it would appear that Paul is warning his readers that certain behaviors must by all means be avoided because they tend to particularly alienate a person from God. Paul could also simply be saying that such sins are a living contradiction of the Lordship of Christ. For Paul, to say "Christian fornicator" makes as much sense as to say "Muslim hog roast." Both are logical contradictions.

Some critics would argue that the New Testament is as outdated as the Old Testament as a source of ethical teaching. They would argue that it was written in a time and culture so different from ours that its prescriptions are no longer valid or relevant for us. Why should our ethical beliefs be dictated by the opinions of some dead Bronze Age Jewish males? Such a skeptical approach bears no resemblance to the Christian doctrine of the authority of Scripture.

A strong case can be made that "Greet one another with a holy kiss" is a New Testament exhortation that is strongly conditioned by the time and culture in which it was uttered. But what about "It is a shame for a man to have long hair" (1 Cor 11:14)? To determine what Paul meant by "long hair," one must take a look at the culture in which he spoke, where crew cuts were only for effeminate boys, and where shoulder-length hair for men was apparently the norm. Where Paul does not permit women to teach or have authority over men (1 Tim 2:12), we may observe that no one but the Pythagoreans, the Epicureans, and the Isis cult put women in any comparable teaching position; in this regard, the first-century Church was in a position much like that of the church in present-day Pakistan, a culture not yet ready for women in religious authority.[2]

However, whenever the ancient cultural situation is much like our own, then God's word to us must be the same as God's word was to them. A key example is the sexuality issue. The New Testament world was characterized by as much sexual freedom, both gay and straight, as we have today, arguably much more. Voices from ancient times (see chapter 4) speak of same-sex love that is mutual, committed, and immutable, despite modern claims that the ancients did not have our understanding of same-sex orientation. One may reject historic Christian teaching on fornication and homosexuality, but one cannot dismiss it as outdated or as any more unrealistic (I would argue, countercultural) than the age in which God spoke these words.

Examining the New Testament sin lists reveals a collection of behaviors that seriously endanger one's relationship with God, and/or potentially exclude a person from the Holy City if one persists in them: murder, illicit sex, theft, idol worship, greed, alcohol abuse, and sorcery involving pharmaceuticals. There is not a single sin on this list (with the possible exception of greed) that today's church would not also consider to be a serious moral issue. As Paul makes clear to the Corinthians, none of these is by any measure the unforgivable sin. Paul's warning goes to those who continue to practice such sins as a lifestyle.

---

2. One may also cite examples of prophetesses such as Deborah (Judg 4:4–8; 5:1–31) and Huldah (2 Kgs 22:14–20) who proclaimed God's word, as well as Phoebe, a "minister" (a *diakonos*, not a "deaconess"—same word that Paul uses to refer to himself) at the church at Cenchreae (Rom 16:1), Priscilla (who helps Aquila correct Apollos's theology in Acts 18:26), and Junia, who was "prominent among the apostles" (Rom 16:7).

Paul indicates in his Romans 1 sin list that all sins are worthy of death. That is true. Some sins are slow killers like carbon monoxide. Some are like cyanide. Both are poisons. But some poisons are more dangerous than others. 1 John 5:16–17 puts sins into categories of "unto death" and not "unto death." While it is unclear exactly what John means, it is clear that he teaches that some sins are much more serious than others.

The Westminster Larger Catechism (7.260–61) teaches that "All transgressions of the law of God are not equally heinous;" they may be aggravated by several factors. A sin may be made worse by the identity of the person who commits the offense, if their faith or position in life makes them an example that is likely to be followed. Another aggravating factor can be the party who is sinned against. The final factor is the nature and quality of the offense. Wishing to kill my neighbor, for example, is a sin that does much less damage to others than carrying out that wish. Even God-less law recognizes the difference between "victimless crimes" and crimes where others get hurt.

The New Testament's sin lists give us echoes of Jesus' teaching on sin. These lists all complement or supplement one another. They fill in each other's gaps. We never find them disagreeing. We never find one list saying "X is bad" and another list saying "X is good." Together, these lists give us a relatively coherent picture of apostolic teaching on sin. Viewed in such a light, the New Testament sin lists present a sober set of boundaries that can be as useful to God's people in the twenty-first century as they were to the age in which they were first written.

The earliest post-biblical sin list gives us a snapshot that summarizes the church's earliest understanding of what all is on God's sin list. Around 95 AD, the *Didache* (the "Teaching of the Twelve Apostles") lists the following sins: murder, adultery, child molestation (*paidophthoreō*), fornication, stealing, magic (*mageuō*), use of potions (*pharmakeuō*), abortion, infanticide, coveting, perjury, false testimony, insults, grudge-holding, greed, swindling, hypocrisy, spite, haughtiness, and hate (*Did.* 2:1–7). Almost every item is a word straight from one of the New Testament sin lists, the exceptions being child molestation (the New Testament uses the generic term for homosexual behavior, *arsenokoitē*), magic, abortion, infanticide, and hate (which is not itemized on any sin list). A similar list is found in *Didache* 5:1. The *Didache* also condemns divination, incantations, and astrology (*mathēmatikos*).

In the next three chapters, we will take a closer look at several of the behaviors and character traits that Jesus and his apostles identified as sin.

4

Sex in the First-Century World

SEX OUTSIDE OF MARRIAGE

SEXUAL IMMORALITY IN THE Roman world was as pervasive as it is today. There was even more sexual freedom (both gay and straight) than we have today. What this means is that God's word to us on the subject carries just as much weight today as it did back then.

The very first item on Jesus' sin list in Mark 7:21–22 is fornication, *porneia* (from which we get our word "pornography"), a word that originally meant "prostitution," but which became a broad term for all kinds of sex outside of marriage between a man and a woman. Jesus puts *porneia* at the top of his sin list, both to reinforce the moral convictions of his Jewish listeners, and also to help his later Gentile followers, who needed to hear this teaching straight from him, because this teaching contradicts their culture (and ours).

Porneia is condemned in the New Testament as an extension of *moicheia* (adultery), one of the Old Testament death penalty crimes. Premarital sex is only explicitly condemned in the Old Testament in the case where a girl is found not to be a virgin when she reaches the marriage bed (Deut 22:13–21). The reason a term for "prostitution" is used here (the term *zanah*, "to play the harlot," is used for all premarital sex in Hebrew) is because there was no swinging singles' scene in ancient Israel, and the issue of whether payment was involved was irrelevant. In most cases, seduction of a virgin was remedied by either marriage, or by payment of the bridewealth to the girl's family, if her father refuses to let the man marry her (Exod 22:16–17).

The pagan male attitude toward sex may be summarized by a quote from Demosthenes: "Courtesans we have for the sake of pleasure, concubines for the daily care (*therapeias*) of the body, wives for having children legitimately" (*Neaer* 59.122). Seneca (a contemporary of Paul's) writes that in his day, "Chastity is simply a proof of ugliness" (*Ben.* 3.16.1–3).

The seventh commandment only specifically forbids adultery, but as the Jews encountered the sexual freedom of the Greeks and Romans, they promptly expanded their understanding of that commandment to include all sex outside of the lifelong bond of marriage. Judaism vociferously rejected the pervasive premarital sex that it saw in the Gentile world. Such strong conviction did not arise out of a vacuum. It is argued here that by forbidding *porneia*, the Jews were simply making explicit what they had always assumed, which we are now forced to do again today in our present debate about sex.

As we saw in chapter 3, the sin that appears on the New Testament sin lists more than any other sin is *porneia*, sex apart from marriage. Every New Testament writer except James rules *porneia* out of bounds (and James probably assumes the prohibition). Avoiding *porneia* is the first lesson in morality that Paul gives the brand-new Christians at Thessalonika after they quit worshipping idols (1 Thess 4:3–8). Paul tells the Corinthians that *porneia* is a sin against one's own body and a violation of the one-flesh relationship for which God created sex (1 Cor 6:16–20). He tells the Ephesians (Eph 5:3) that *porneia* should not even be considered as a valid Christian lifestyle option.

Dale Martin says it's unrealistic to expect young people to remain virgins until age thirty.[1] (It's probably just as unrealistic for them to stay off of recreational drugs, too, although we have extremely little biblical teaching to oppose that evil. And which evil presents more danger to the human psyche, sex or drugs?) The real question is, what are we willing to do to make it easier or more advantageous for our people to marry earlier? And why don't we get rid of the outdated practice of paying survivor's benefits and start paying widowed persons of both genders a lump sum that won't have to be sacrificed if one remarries?

So Dale Martin can spare us all the statistics about illicit sex. We might as well talk about how many of our pastors, elders, and deacons have tried marijuana, meth, and cocaine. I don't care who has tried them, or even who used to be addicted to them, but I do care about who's still using them. And even if 90 percent of our people have used recreational drugs, that doesn't mean we should capitulate to the cultural stampede. (By that logic, we should restore all those ministers we have defrocked for misconduct, if they add up to 20 percent or more of all pastors.)

1. Martin, "Sex," 4.

As for the question of whether we pursue a "don't ask, don't tell" approach toward sexually active singles, perhaps that is the (well-meaning, but possibly misguided?) attempt of some of us to give God time to change people's hearts. I don't want to know about my colleague's cocaine habit, but if it becomes impossible to ignore, we have to deal with it, especially if they've been elected to serve on our ruling board. "Don't ask, don't tell" doesn't work for incest, pedophilia, or domestic violence, because the harm involved is unacceptable and intolerable by any standard. Hidden fornication (heterosexual or homosexual) may be nothing more than self-inflicted harm, therefore it may be easier to look the other way from, but when fornication becomes self-affirming and demands acceptance in the name of "justice," then it becomes a case of gangrene in the body of Christ. "Whoever says 'I know him' and does not keep his commands is a liar, and the truth is not in them" (1 John 2:4).

What about cohabitation? Judith Krantz, who thought that fornication was just fine, knew what was wrong with cohabitation when she wrote her article "Living Together Is a Rotten Idea."[2] Her arguments are just as valid today as they were thirty years ago: keeping a separate roof over your head helps keep you from getting sucked into making a bad decision about marriage. I would add to Krantz's arguments: I have observed that couples who live together because they are afraid of marital commitment, are setting themselves up for the same pain they want to avoid, by their intimate (i.e. sexual) involvement. According to Paul, God's Superglue ("the two shall become one flesh") works either way, married or not. What difference does "a piece of paper" make? Answer: What sensible person would put down $150,000 on a house, without a "piece of paper" which states that the house now belongs to them?

HOMOSEXUALITY

Arsenokoitai is a word first used (probably coined) by Paul as a translation of the words "those (masculine) who have *koitos* with a male" in Leviticus. *Arsenokoitai* is a purely generic term, with no abusive relationship implied, although pro-gay scholars such as John Boswell have claimed otherwise. Homosexual behavior (both male and female) is also the shocker on Paul's portrait of human depravity in Romans 1:26–27. Homosexuality also seems to be alluded to by a code term on the sin list in Revelation 22:8 ("dogs"), harking back to Deuteronomy 23:18, "You

2. Krantz, "Living Together," 218–27.

shall not bring the fee of a prostitute or the wages of a male prostitute (literally: a dog) into the house of the Lord."

The other term for homosexual behavior on Paul's sin list in 1 Corinthians 6:9 is *malakoi*, literally "soft ones." It is the term for the passive or receptive partner in a homosexual act between two males. Contrary to the claim that the only sin condemned in same-sex sexual activity is abuse or exploitation, the fact that *malakoi* are also included on Paul's sin list is an indication that it is the act itself and not the abuse of power or exploitation that is the sin in question.

Jesus and other Jewish sources in the New Testament assume the validity of the Mosaic law on this subject and apparently felt no need to be more explicit on what they considered to be an uncomfortable subject. Nevertheless, on his sin list in Mark, Jesus includes the term *aselgeia*, a term used by Jews to refer to the most shocking sex crimes forbidden in the Torah (since Jesus has already named fornication and adultery on this list, he is most likely referring to homosexual behavior, incest, and bestiality).[3] *Aselgeia* is used ten times in the New Testament, including Romans 13:13, 2 Corinthians 12:21, Ephesians 4:19, 1 Peter 4:3, 2 Peter 2:7, and Jude 4. Notably, it is never used where *arsenokoitai* is used.

The final two words for out-of-bounds sexual behavior in the New Testament are *koitē* and *akatharsia*. *Koitē* is a slang term that means literally "bed." It is a neutral term, but is used in Romans 13 instead of *porneia* to refer to sexual promiscuity. *Akatharsia* is a generic term that means literally "uncleanness," but which appears to be a reference to all sexual sins that defile more than just at the ritual level. Any sexual act defiled a person until the next sundown, according to the Mosaic law, but a sin such as adultery defiles the person in a way that neither ritual bath nor sacrifice can wash away. Such is true for all of the death-penalty sexual offenses, and is most probably what Paul means by *akatharsia* in passages such as Ephesians 4:19.

ARGUMENTS IN FAVOR OF HOMOSEXUAL BEHAVIOR

What about arguments used to defend homosexual behavior for Christians? The story of David and Jonathan is the only scripture that requires any explanation. The story of David and Jonathan (where David sings in 2 Sam 1:26, "Your love for me was wonderful, surpassing the love of women") is designed to prove the opposite of what is claimed.

3. See Hobson, "*Aselgeia*," 65–74.

The most this passage could possibly prove is that these two men were bi-sexual (David's heterosexual lust overpowers his senses in 2 Samuel 11). But even this conclusion is highly unlikely. In a context where an apologist for David is trying to exonerate David of trying to wrench the kingdom away from Saul, David is portrayed as possessing a love for Saul's son that is not blinded by romance or erotic desire. Hebrew culture presumes that such romance or eroticism would be heterosexual; the whole argument made by the biblical writer depends on this assumption.

The centurion's slave whom Jesus healed was the man's gay lover, we are told? If so, it was an unequal relationship. But the claim is a fantasy. So are the claims of a sexual relationship between Jesus and John ("the disciple whom Jesus loved"), or between Ruth and Naomi.

"Times have changed," we are told. "People back then had no concept of inborn, loving, mutual same-sex behavior." Not so! The New Testament period was full of normalized, loving, mutual homosexual behavior. Plato declared homosexuality the noblest form of love. Many believed it was ordained by God, such as Aristophanes in Plato's *Symposium*, where Aristophanes speaks of men who are "born" to be "the willing mate of a man" (192B), and when two such men find each other, "the two of them are wondrously thrilled with affection and intimacy and love, and are hardly to be induced to leave each other's side for a single moment," and if Hephaestus should offer to weld them together forever to share a single life both here and in Hades, the two would gladly consent, this being what they had always yearned for (192D-E). Aristophanes concludes that the way to happiness is "to give our love its true fulfilment: let every one find his own favourite, and so revert to his primal estate." (193C)

During Roman times, Callicratidas makes a speech worthy of "Brokeback Mountain", where he pledges lifelong undying love for his male lover, and calls for their ashes to be mixed together after death:

> I pray that it may for ever be my lot to sit opposite my dear one and hear close to me his sweet voice, to go out when he goes out and share every activity with him. But, if . . . illness should lay its hold on him, I shall ail with him when he is weak, and, when he puts out to sea through stormy waves, I shall sail with him. And, should a violent tyrant bind him in chains, I shall put the same fetters around myself . . . Should I see bandits or foemen rushing upon him, I would arm myself even beyond my strength, and if he

dies, I shall not bear to live. I shall give final instructions to those
I love next best after him to pile up a common tomb for both of
us, to unite my bones with his and not keep even our dumb ashes
apart from each other." (Pseudo-Lucian, *Erōtēs* 46.4–10)

Callicratidas calls this "the honourable love inbred in us from
childhood," and asks, "Why then do you censure this as being an exotic
indulgence of our time, though it is an ordinance enacted by divine laws
and a heritage that has come down to us?" (48.2–3)

More quotes from Callicratidas: ". . . love of males (*ho arrēn erōs*), I
say, is the only activity combining both pleasure and virtue." (31.1) "For
marriage is a remedy invented to ensure man's necessary perpetuity, but
only love for males is a noble duty enjoined by a philosophic spirit." (33:1)
"Let no one expect love of males in early times" (35:1), says Callicratidas,
because intercourse with women was necessary to preserve the species,
but love of males is superior because it came after humans had leisure for
thought (35:5). That's why Callicratidas argues that animals do not have
such love, because they are just beasts, but "for men wisdom coupled with
knowledge has chosen what is best, and has formed the opinion that love
between males is the most stable (*bebaiotatous*, "steadfast" or "secure") of
loves" (36.10).

Callicratidas rejects the company of women: "Let women be ci-
phers and be retained merely for childbearing; but in all else away with
them, and may I be rid of them!" (38.5) He then goes on trash women
for their ugliness and all their attempts to adorn themselves. In the
same way, Plutarch (*Erōtikos* 750C) narrates a speech by Protogones,
who claims, "Genuine love has no connexion whatsoever with the
women's quarters. I deny that it is love that you have felt for women
and girls . . ." Instead, he says, such love is "effeminate and bastard" and
should be forbidden as unmasculine: "But that other lax and house-
bound love, that spends its time in the bosoms and beds of women,
ever pursuing a soft life, enervated amid pleasure devoid of manliness
and friendship and inspiration—it should be proscribed."

Times have not changed! Greco-Roman culture knew about beliefs
in homosexual orientation and mutual homosexual love that were very
much like the beliefs advocated by today's progressives. In this context,
the New Testament's command against unchastity in all of its forms was
totally scandalous and unreasonable.

To argue that same-sex desire is part of God's good creation is a tragic mistake. Same-sex relations are a part of nature. But so are black widows and praying mantises who kill and eat their mates, and mackerel who kill purely for sport. "Go and do thou likewise"? And again, why is the natural sexual attraction to children not a part of God's good creation? No, we cannot lump homosexuality and pedophilia together, but why is the person who is attracted to children to be viewed as dirt, while everyone else is loved by God?

The real issue is not whether those who practice same-sex intercourse are loved by God, but the fact that they are both grieving God and harming themselves. If we want to argue from nature, Budziszewski argues from God's design: Our lungs were designed to take in air, not food. A steering wheel is designed to steer the car, and its purpose explains why the car has one. If a steering wheel fails to accomplish its purpose, the fault does not rest in the designer.[4]

It is no mistake that God's design requires a man and a woman. Both man and woman equally reflect the image of God. But neither of us does so completely. So when we try to unite two persons of the same gender together in a one-flesh relationship, part of God's image is missing. It is therefore not surprising that in most same-sex relationships, we still find echoes of masculine-feminine pairing. We are attracted to the part of God's image that we find missing in ourselves. Homosexually oriented persons, like the rest of us, have God-given needs for love and affirmation from their own gender, needs for which sex is not the answer.

THE CENTRAL TEACHING OF SCRIPTURE

The historical Jesus affirmed only celibacy and committed marriage between a man and woman. If Jesus actually believed otherwise, he was in an unparalleled position to correct the human race once and for all on this subject.

We find the Bible's central teaching on sexuality in three key places: in the creation story in the Torah (Gen 2:24), reaffirmed clearly by Jesus (Matt 19:3–6 = Mark 10:6–9), and reaffirmed a third time by Paul (1 Cor 6:16; Eph 5:31): *"the two* (man and woman) *shall become one flesh."* Genesis, Jesus, and Paul clearly teach one consistent biblical sexual ethic. This teaching is enunciated a total of three times, in the teaching of three

4. Budziszewski, *What We Can't Not Know*, 106; 110.

leading authorities (the Torah, Jesus, and Paul), and it is presented in contexts where it is treated as foundational, not as a stray detail. The teaching serves as a coherent core that supports and explains the Bible's prohibitions on fornication, adultery, incest, homosexual behavior, and bestiality, while also serving as a corrective judgment on behavior in the Bible that appears otherwise to be condoned. Cases of polygamy[5] and prostitution in the Bible give rise to the common but false claim that the Bible affirms multiple contradictory teachings on sex. These diverse practices that are narrated in Scripture are not to be equated with what Scripture actually teaches as God's design.

"The two (man and woman) shall become one flesh." The alleged multiple sexual teachings in the Bible are not teachings at all, they are departures, often teaching us by negative example. The centrality of the one-flesh sexual union even comes through in the incest legislation in Leviticus, where whole classes of potential partners are ruled out because these partners are "your own flesh" (*she'ēr besarō*—Lev 18:6), including even in-laws. (That chapter, by the way, makes it a nightmare to even consider polygamy, with all the in-laws that one is forbidden to marry.) Dale Patrick points out in his comments on homosexual behavior in the Holiness Code: "Perhaps it was believed that the sexual drive was meant to unite man and woman (so Gen. 2:23, 24), and any other expression of it violated its purpose."[6] Indeed, it was.

God created sex to unite two lives, not to be an expression of transient passion. God created sex as the spiritual equivalent of Superglue: it binds two people together too intimately to rip them apart without causing needless pain. As Paul argues, even a few minutes in a "love" motel is enough to create this bond (1 Cor 6:16). It is this truth that prompts Jesus to utter his most scandalous teaching on divorce, a teaching that never would have been invented by the early church (E. P. Sanders calls it "the best-attested tradition in the gospels"). The issue is not whether remarriage is permitted (Jesus presumes remarriage in Matt 5:32). The issue is the violation of God's one-flesh intention, which can never be

5. The Bible's toleration of polygamy may be explained in that it involves marriage, and therefore affirms a lifelong one-flesh union. But God commanded that the *two* shall become one, not three or more partners. Paul writes that a church leader must be literally a "one-wife man" (1 Tim 3:2; Tit 1:6). The Roman ideal viewed remarriage, even after widowhood, as a form of sexual indulgence. Because Paul commanded younger widows to remarry (1 Tim 5:14), it is likely that "one-wife man" is merely intended to rule out polygamy.

6. Patrick, *Law*, 139.

better than a lesser of evils. Try as we may, Jesus says, we cannot erase a sexual relationship.

One may also take note that, by his application of "the two shall become one," Jesus implicitly rules out polygamy and prostitution. So much for the supposed multiple sexual teachings of the Bible! Jesus also never overturns prohibitions against sexual immorality in Leviticus or anywhere in the Torah; in fact, he is more demanding than the Torah. And the fact that Jesus ate with sexual sinners does not mean he was soft on sexual sin, any more than his eating with crooks means that Jesus was soft on economic exploitation. To completely deconstruct the myth of the inclusive Jesus, go to the chapter on "The Witness of Jesus" in Robert Gagnon's excellent resource, *The Bible and Homosexual Practice* (see bibliography).

What is meant by the biblical teaching of the one-flesh union created by a sexual relationship? Here we must use our theological imaginations. One way we can visualize this union is biologically: DNA is transferred, and two bodies are joined into a unit that requires parts of both male and female, parts that were made for one another. Another way we can visualize this union is emotional: sexual intercourse causes the release of the hormone oxytocin, which creates or enhances an emotional bond of intimacy between the partners, an effect that works to keep the couple together and causes emotional pain when the relationship is broken.[7] That's what Jesus was talking about when he says, "What God has joined together, let no one separate." That's also why the body of Christ needs to do what we can to discourage the premature formation of such intimate relationships outside the context of lifelong marriage. As Josh McDowell tells young people, "No one has invented a condom for the mind," that is, a device to protect the heart from broken sexual relationships that were never meant to be.

IS THE BIBLE'S SEXUAL ETHIC UNREASONABLE?

The logic that it is unreasonable to require celibacy as the only alternative to heterosexual marriage breaks down when applied to those who are sexually attracted to children: why is celibacy reasonable only for them? This is not to equate pedophilia with homosexuality. The point is: if we must refrain from a natural desire because it is not good for us, then we must do so even if all parties involved are consenting adults. The

---

7. See Harris, "Casual Sex," 315.

Bible is clear that the lifelong one-flesh union of a man and a woman is the only healthy place for sexual intimacy.

But, it is objected, the Bible's sexual ethic is entirely based on the concepts of male supremacy and women as men's possessions. Regardless of whether the biblical writers believed in male supremacy or that women were the property of men, the biblical teaching on sexuality neither contains, presumes, nor requires such concepts. How can we become "one flesh" with someone who is merely our property?

It is asked, "Why is the Church wasting so much time and so many resources fighting about sex?" The answer is because so much effort and resources are being expended to ram a hole through a central Christian moral teaching at precisely this point. Can you imagine if all this effort was being used to force recreational drugs upon the Church? Can you imagine us being asked to exercise the utmost in forbearance toward the puffing of reefers around the Table? After all, our hang-up about drugs (see chapter 5) has much less biblical basis than our hang-ups about *porneia* and *arsenokoitia*.

"Being in Christ" changes everything, we are told. Indeed, it does. But that doesn't mean that core ethical teachings of Scripture go out the window. What Paul says about being in Christ in 2 Corinthians 5:17 and Galatians 3:26–28, must be read in context of what he says in 1 Corinthians 6:9–11 and Galatians 5:16–21. He says in these two passages that fornication, adultery, *aselgeia*, and *arsenokoitia* (a generic term for same-sex intercourse) jeopardize our status in that supposedly inclusive body of Christ. This same Paul goes on to say that it is impossible to join a part of Christ's body to a prostitute (paid or unpaid). Does this means we are saved, not by grace, but by avoiding illicit sex? Clearly not, but at the very least, Paul is clearly rejecting the brand of inclusiveness preached by the pro-gay-sex crowd.

OTHER BOUNDARIES TO BE CONSIDERED

Other than keeping sex in the context of a lifelong relationship between a man and a woman, where else do we draw the line? Within marriage, partners are free to follow their consciences together as they express their love for one another. We only need to rule out the intentional infliction of pain or emotional discomfort on our spouse.

What about the issue of procreation within marriage? Some who wish to caricature the Bible's sexual ethic claim that those who practice birth control or those who are infertile or too old to conceive children are violating biblical standards. Such a claim is an exaggeration. The Bible nowhere teaches, commands, or requires that sex must be capable of producing children in order to be morally good.

Yet the attitude that sex is only allowed for procreation is found frequently in the early church. Clement of Alexandria writes around 200 AD, "The seed is not to be vainly ejaculated, nor is it to be damaged, nor is it to be wasted" (*Paed.* 2.10.91.2). Therefore, he says, Moses forbids sex during menstruation, lest "what is soon to become a man" be ritually polluted. Likewise, Clement argues that both masturbation and sex during pregnancy are forbidden, because in both cases the seed is wasted.

The early church's position on this issue is based on a misconception that the male sperm already contains a complete human individual, like a plant seed that merely needs to germinate when planted. The advent of the microscope corrected this misunderstanding by revealing that a true individual human life is not created until both egg and sperm combine in conception. This discovery removes early church objections to sex that does not lead to procreation.

As for intimacy short of marriage (i. e., how far is too far to go on a date?), I have always used the general logic: if you can't show it in public, it's off limits to the public. It belongs only in the hands of your future spouse. Intimacy in private areas, even if it stops short of intercourse, is too intimate until a couple makes a binding, lifelong commitment.

In the Sermon on the Mount, Jesus extends God's teaching on sex beyond physical activity to activity in our minds. While it is always worse to act on sinful desires than to merely think them, Jesus makes it clear that the thought also counts. It is thoughts that ultimately give rise to actions.

The noun *epithymia*, the word often translated "lust," is used thirty-eight times in the New Testament. The related verb form, *epithymeō*, is used an additional sixteen times. The verb is the verb that the Septuagint translation uses in the tenth commandment, "Thou shalt not *covet.*" *Epithymia* is the basic word for "desire." It is the word Paul uses in Philippians 1:23 where he says, "My desire is to depart and be with Christ." It is the word Jesus uses in Luke 22:15 where he says, "I have earnestly desired to eat this Passover with you before I suffer." In 1 Timothy 3:1, Paul writes, "If anyone aspires to the office of overseer, he *desires* a noble task." Most of the times this word is used, the meaning is ambiguous. In fact, there are only six times that this noun or verb is used where the meaning is undoubtedly sexual: Matthew 5:28, Romans 1:24, 1 Thessalonians 4:5, 1 Peter 4:3, and 2 Peter 2:10 and 2:18.

Matthew 5:28, however, is central to what we're talking about: "Whoever looks at a woman to desire her, has already committed adultery in his heart." There is no superior virtue in adultery in the head versus adultery in the bed, even though acting on the wish causes far more damage to multiple parties. The wish proves that we are not holier than the person who carries out the wish.

More importantly, however, adultery in the mind interferes with our relationship with our present (or future) spouse. This is particularly true for pornography: one spouse ends up being compared with images with which it may be impossible for a real-life spouse to compete. But the same principle is also true when we allow ourselves to compare our spouse's body with the real-life bodies of others, creating attachments in the mind that interfere with our marital relationship at both the physical and emotional levels.

Lust should not be automatically equated with autoerotic behavior. To some extent, the release of sexual tension does not absolutely require the desire to possess specific persons via pictures or imagination. If this behavior was a priority on God's sin list, God would likely have spelled this out in writing.[8] Onan's sin that prompted such a severe judgment from God was not that he spilled semen on the ground and thereby wasted it (Gen 38:8–10), but the fact that he took pleasure from his brother's widow while denying descendants to his brother, a crime particularly hideous in Hebrew eyes.

Autoeroticism may even find an appropriate place within a marriage relationship with the consent of both spouses, as long as it supports rather than subtracts from their love relationship. For those who are single, autoeroticism is a thousand times preferable to sexual involvement with a person outside of marriage, because it does not involve a one-flesh relationship and all the perils of involvement in a relationship that will not endure. The problems are that it is still difficult to keep lust out of autoeroticism, and that autoeroticism can often inflame desire rather than satisfying it (like drinking salt water for thirst).

---

8. However, Collins (*Ethics*, 65–70) argues extensively that in his teaching about cutting off the eye or hand that leads us to sin, Jesus is echoing the strong official condemnation of masturbation by the rabbis in the Talmud.

The progressive wing of the church wishes to argue that the only sexual boundaries whose violations call for discipline against a church leader are sex with someone who is under age, and sex with a subordinate (such as a pastor with a parishioner, or the like). In both cases, a relationship with inequality of power is involved.

While this moral principle is valid as far as it goes, it does not go far enough. Those who advocate the principle, fail to apply it to entertainment or sports celebrities and their fans, which are relationships that are usually even more unequal. The principle also lacks direct biblical grounding. Nowhere is sex forbidden in Scripture because someone is under another person's authority, or is too young. The central teaching of Scripture on sexuality is a better way to rule out inappropriate relationships. If sex is reserved solely for marriage between a man and a woman, questions of age and power become ultimately irrelevant, although the wisdom of relationships where there is too great a difference in age or power may need to be examined.

No, "historical scholarship" has not overthrown the historic teaching of God's word on sexuality, although it has tried valiantly. Historical scholarship will show that Christian sexual morality was radically counter-cultural in a Rome that would make San Francisco look Puritan. Whatever God said to a culture that was so much like ours in the area of sexuality, must be the same as what God says to us. When God speaks such scandalous words to a culture with even more sexual "freedom" than our own, then when God calls that culture to reject all sex outside a loving lifetime one-flesh relationship between a man and a woman, God's word to us must be the same as God's word was to them.

5

Alcohol and Drugs in the First-Century World

HOW MUCH DOES THE BIBLE REALLY SAY?

WHILE I WAS A teenage Christian in the 1970s, one of my friends tried to persuade me from the Bible that it was okay for a Christian to get high on marijuana. His proof? 1 Timothy 4:4: "Everything created by God is good, and nothing is to be rejected if it is received with thanksgiving." (I should have answered, "Yes! God gave us marijuana, not to smoke it, but to make rope out of it!") Another friend who tried to reconcile marijuana and his faith ended up changing his mind, based on Romans 14:23, "Whatever does not proceed from faith is sin." These examples illustrate the fact that the Bible's case against the use of mind-altering drugs is not as slam-dunk as we might have imagined, when we start looking for specific texts that address the issue.

While modern Western nations rarely forbid sexual offenses such as fornication or adultery by law, for some reason, they tend to deal much more severely with the use of hallucinatory drugs, opiates, and cocaine. Laws against substance abuse are of fairly recent origin. One searches the ancient world in vain for such laws, other than the prohibition of wine in the Quran (which has been extended to an outright ban on all alcoholic beverages in some countries). And even though there are movements to decriminalize the use of some drugs, and even though some local laws are comparatively lenient toward certain drugs, today's consensus in favor of anti-drug laws is surprisingly strong in view of the fact that there is comparatively little anti-drug Judeo-Christian or other moral teaching on which it is based. The fact that the mind-altering effects of alcohol, marijuana, and opium were known to the biblical world (cocaine was not known until contact with South America, and methamphetamine had not yet been invented) should also be kept in mind as we examine what God has said on substance abuse.

ALCOHOL IN THE BIBLE

Drunkenness carried no penalty in the Old Testament, merely censure. Proverbs 20:1 says, "Wine is a mocker, beer is a brawler, and whoever is led astray by it is not wise." Both Noah and Lot end up in trouble when they place themselves under the influence of alcohol (Gen 9:20–21; 19:30–36). Eli says to Hannah, "How long will you be drunken? Put away your wine!" (1 Sam 1:14) The Law of Moses commands priests, "Drink no wine nor beer, neither you nor your sons, when you enter the tent of meeting, lest you die." (Lev 10:9) The message here is that priests must be careful not to make mistakes that would put them in danger of the wrath of God, therefore they must not be under the influence of alcohol when they come on duty.

Similarly, King Lemuel's mother (Prov 31:4–5) says, "It is not for kings to drink wine, nor for rulers to desire beer, or else they will drink and forget what has been decreed, and will pervert all the rights of the afflicted." Yet Lemuel's mother also says, "Give beer to one who is perishing, and wine to those in bitter distress; let them drink and forget their poverty, and remember their misery no more." (Prov 31:6–7) While we may not wish to recommend alcohol as a means of forgetting one's personal troubles, we may see in this passage a precedent for giving morphine to patients who are in severe physical pain.

The New Testament recognizes drunkenness as a threat to one's spiritual health. Substance abuse appears on the New Testament sin lists both as alcohol abuse (*methusoi*—1 Cor 6:10) and as *pharmakeia*, a form of witchcraft involving the use of drugs, potions, and poisons. Together, these two concepts form the entire New Testament case against substance abuse, which is much slimmer than its case against sexual immorality. One can only imagine how the church would have to scramble to defend itself biblically, if we faced a crowd who demanded the right to marijuana and cocaine at the table of the Lord, rather than a crowd that demands ordination for those who practice fornication and same-sex intercourse as a lifestyle.

The key verse on substance abuse for Christians is Ephesians 5:18, "Do not be drunk (*methuō*) with wine." The reason given is because drunkenness leads to *asōtia*, a term that is hard to define in simple language, partly because our translations use words like "dissipation," "debauchery," and "profligacy," words that are equally hard to put into plain English. Let's take a look at how this word is used elsewhere in the Bible.

Asōtia is used a total of four times in the New Testament. As an adverb, it appears in the parable of the Prodigal Son in Luke 15:13, where the son spends all his money in "riotous" (*asōtōs*) living. In 1 Peter 4:3–4, *asōtia* is used as a catch-all term to refer to "licentiousness (*aselgeia*), lusts, drunkenness, orgies, drinking parties, and lawless idolatry," a lifestyle that is out of control. And in Titus 1:6, Paul urges that church leaders be chosen whose children are not open to charges of *asōtia*. Outside the New Testament, *asōtia* is one of four evil spirits named in *Testament of Judah* 16:2, along with lust, burning (wrath?), and shameful gain.

The basic idea of *asōtia* is to create a mess of one's life by out-of-control indulgence, somewhat like our expression of getting (literally) "wasted." How to capture all that in a single English word? Perhaps we may translate Ephesians 5:18, "Do not get drunk with wine, because that is a reckless, harmful, degrading form of excess."

Paul's command applies not just to wine, but to other mind-altering chemicals. The reason that other drinks or mind-altering drugs are not named specifically by Paul here is because none of these other alternatives is being abused at Ephesus; the specific problem is over-use of wine, perhaps in imitation of the Dionysius cult, perhaps for simple escape from one's personal pain. Paul insists that the alternative to being under the influence of alcohol is to be under the influence of (literally "filled with") the Holy Spirit, for which the use of mind-altering drugs of any kind is a dangerous substitute. Instead of being controlled by the Holy Spirit of God, getting high on chemicals such as alcohol opens us to the control of spirits that are not from God. That's where the concept of *pharmakeia* contributes to our discussion of substance abuse.

Pharmakeia was a word with three different meanings that were all lumped together in the mind of the average Greek-speaker. It could mean the use of drugs, poisons, and/or witchcraft. *Pharmakeia* was illegal under Roman law (partly because it often involved the poisoning of others), and any kind of witchcraft was punishable by death under Mosaic law. (*Pharmakeia* is always used in the Greek Old Testament to translate the term "witchcraft.")

MEDICINE IN THE ANCIENT WORLD

The use of drugs, as well as the medical profession as a whole, was viewed with considerable skepticism if not fear by the people of the Roman world, both Jews and pagans. Even the best doctors in the first century AD were quacks by modern standards, and at worst, the public feared that they would be given poison by their doctors. The early Christian Tatian (170 AD) trashed all doctors and medicine (*Oration* 18:1). The rabbis said (*m. Qidd.* 4:14), "The best among physicians is destined for Gehenna (hell)," which shows a general attitude in Palestine that doctors were quacks. But Sirach 38:1 says, "Honor the physician with the honor due him, for God created him." Sirach goes on to say, "From the earth God produces medicines, and a sensible man should not reject them" (Sir 38:4). Sirach writes in Egypt, where the medical profession had a higher reputation. Yet from Egypt also came the Jewish philosopher Philo, who complains that people run to doctors and drugs because they lack faith in God (*Sacr.* 19:70–71).[1]

The Greek physician Galen believed that "drugs are just like the hands of the gods."[2] Likewise, Plato (*Resp.* 459c) preferred more "masculine" doctors who knew how to use drugs in their practice.

While most of the drugs and other treatments used in the ancient world were of questionable value at best, there were two drugs that were known to the ancients that are well-known today for their power to influence the human mind. Let's take a look at them.

OPIUM AND MARIJUANA

Opium was commonly used to kill pain in biblical times. The Sumerians (pre-2000 BC) called it HUL.GIL, "the joy plant." The Ebers Papyrus (Egypt, 1550 BC) prescribed opium to quiet a crying child (an extra-strength equivalent of Num-Zit?). It was also prescribed by Hippocrates to relieve the pain of childbirth. Opium seems to be the drug called *nēpenthes* by Homer (*Od.* 4:219-232), a drug that was drunk with wine to remove all pains and worries. The emperor Marcus Aurelius was well-known to be addicted to opium, who used it to calm his nerves. The

---

1. Amundsen (*Medicine,* 127–57) documents how except for Tatian, virtually all other early Christian writers, including Tertullian and Clement of Alexandria, spoke favorably of doctors and medicine.

2. Galen, *De compositione medicamentorum secundum locus* 6.8, quoted in Amundsen, *Medicine,* 168.

first century AD Greek doctor Dioscorides (*Mat. med.* 4.64.3) noted that opium overdose could be fatal. The only mention of opium in ancient Judaism is from the Jerusalem Talmud (post-200 AD), where it says, "An opium drink [prepared by a gentile] is dangerous." (j. ʿ*Abod. Zar.* 2:2H, Neusner edition)

Marijuana was known in biblical times, but was not as commonly used as opium for its mind-altering effects. Marijuana first appears in the Sumerian language (pre-2000 BC) as ^{šam}A.ZAL.LA. It was known also to the Assyrians of the seventh century BC as *azallu*. The Assyrians are the first to call the hemp plant by the name *qunnabu*, from which we get the Greek/Latin name *K/Cannabis*. Cannabis was used by the Assyrians as an ingredient in incense, and as "a drug where there is depression of spirits."[3] In one Assyrian text, it is also prescribed to treat impotence, yet the Greek scholar Pliny believed that cannabis decreases rather than increases sexual desire (*Nat.* 20.97: "Its seed is said to make the genitals impotent"—likewise, Dioscorides writes in *Peri Hyles Iatrikes* that cannabis seeds, "when eaten in excess, diminish sexual potency"). The price of cannabis in Assyria (571 BC) is reported to have been one pound for three shekels of silver, a price that would seem to reflect its value as a fiber rather than as incense or a drug.[4] Cannabis was also known in Egypt as *smsm.t*, where it was also used in incense, as an oral medication, and as an eye medication.

Pseudo-Plutarch (second century AD) mentions that the people of Thrace used an herb like oregano, threw the tops into their fire after meals, breathed the smoke, got drunk, and fell into a deep sleep.[5] The Greek historian Herodotus (fifth century BC) tells us that the inhabitants of islands in the Araxes River got drunk on the smoke of an unidentified fruit (1.202). In another passage (4.74–75), Herodotus tells us that the Scythians of 450 BC had a custom of throwing cannabis seeds onto red-hot stones after the death of a king and getting drunk by breathing the smoke. The fact that Herodotus knows what cannabis is, throws doubt on whether the unidentified fruit is also cannabis, but in all of the Greco-Roman writers, only Herodotus (and possibly Pseudo-Plutarch) know of cannabis being used as a recreational drug.

3. Thompson, *Dictionary*, 220.

4. Thompson, *Dictionary*, 222n1.

5. Pseudo-Plutarch, *Rivers*, 3.2.1151D–E.

The Greek physician Galen (Kühn edition, 12.8) says that cannabis seed may be used to relieve intestinal gas and earache, and if eaten in excess, it "quenches sexual potency." Galen (Kühn edition, 6.550) also mentioned fried cannabis seeds mixed into desserts: "The seed creates a feeling of warmth, and—if consumed in large amounts—affects the head by sending to it a warm and toxic vapor." In the fourth century BC, Ephippus (Kock edition, fragment 13) includes cannabis on a list of delicacies including wheat-and-honey cakes, nuts, and snails. The personal doctor of the emperor Julian writes that cannabis seed "harms the head" and creates a "warm feeling."[6]

Hemp is not mentioned by the Jews until the Talmud in the fifth century AD (*b. ʿAbod. Zar.* 74b), where the focus is not on any medicinal value of the plant, but simply whether it can be planted mixed with other crops. Although it has been suggested that the Hebrew *qaneh-bosem* (note the similarity in sound to the name "cannabis") may refer to marijuana in the recipe for sacred incense in Exodus 30:33, scholars are generally agreed that this plant is sweet cane. The curious Hebrew term *pannag* in Ezekiel 27:17 (possibly connected to the Sanskrit *bhanga* and Persian *bang*, both meaning cannabis) is a more likely candidate for hemp, although even if so, all we learn was that it was a commodity for which Tyre traded with Judah.

What we learn from the evidence on cannabis in biblical times is that the plant was known, and to some extent its mind-altering effects were known, but it evidently did not play enough of a role in the lives of the biblical audience to warrant any comment or warning against its effects, unlike wine, which played a major role in the lives of those to whom God's word was addressed and was often abused. The same may be said for the lack of mention of opium in biblical texts.

The only mention of drugs in the Bible comparable to drugs that are commonly abused today is where Jesus refuses the drug (*cholē*, "gall") he was offered by the soldiers who crucified him (Matt 27:34), a drug which was probably either opium, hemlock, or absinthe (= biblical "wormwood," a close relative of hemlock), judging from the term's use in the Greek Old Testament in passages such as Psalm 69:21. The Roman soldiers offered Jesus this drug for humanitarian reasons, to spare him from suffering. Opium, or absinthe (if that's what it was), would have

---

6. Quoted in Brunner, "Marijuana," 223.

numbed the pain; hemlock would have quickly put him out of his misery entirely, thus by-passing the torture of hanging from a cross.

In the parallel passage in Mark 15:23, we are told that the wine Jesus was offered was mixed with myrrh. The Talmud (*b. Sanh.* 43a) states that according to Jewish tradition, "When one is led out to execution, he is given a goblet of wine containing a grain of frankincense, in order to benumb his senses." Dioscorides (*Mat. med.* 1.64.3) mentions the narcotic effects (*karōtikēn*) of myrrh. He also says (1.68.3) that frankincense can cause madness if used by a healthy person, and when mixed with wine can cause death. While the Talmud's memory helps confirm the likelihood that Jesus was offered some sort of narcotic at the cross, we can believe Mark's testimony as to the specific drug that was offered to Jesus. We cannot be sure whether Jesus was offered both "gall" and myrrh, or whether Matthew used the term "gall" symbolically as an echo of the prophecy in Psalm 69:21.

Whatever he was offered, Jesus refused to take upon himself the penalty of hell for the entire human race in a state where he would be unable to experience the pain he had to endure. One may argue that Jesus' situation at the cross was unlike any situation that we would ever face. Yet Jesus' determination to face the dreaded pain of hell with full possession of his faculties may still serve as an inspiration to us at times when we are tempted to flee from necessary pain.

THE PROPER USE OF ALCOHOL AND DRUGS

Concerning the use of wine and other alcoholic beverages, the Bible's teaching is that of temperance rather than abstinence. Although technology for preserving non-alcoholic grape juice had been discovered by one Roman writer 200 years before Christ who achieved the feat by sealing the juice in a jug and keeping it submerged in a lake,[7] grape juice did not survive for long in non-alcoholic form in biblical times. Paul advises Timothy to use a little wine for the sake of his stomach (1 Tim 5:23). Fee cites the Talmud (*b. Ber.* 51a; *b. B. Bat.* 58b), Hippocrates (*Vet. med.* 13), Plutarch (*Tu. san.*), and Pliny (*Nat.* 2.19) as support for the medical use of wine in the ancient world, especially for stomach problems.[8] In the

7. Cato, *Agr.* 120.1: "If you wish to keep grape juice through the whole year, put the grape juice in an amphora, seal the stopper with pitch, and sink in the pond. Take it out after thirty days; it will remain sweet the whole year."

8. Fee, *Timothy, Titus*, 94.

Torah (Deut 14:26), Israelites are invited to celebrate God's goodness in the holy city with wine, beer (*shēker*, "strong drink," literally "that which makes drunk"), or whatever they wish.

The Bible does warn us, however, to avoid the use of any alcoholic beverage to where it becomes a mind-impairing drug. In the case of "hard liquor," it would seem to be difficult to consume any great amount of it, except by heavily diluting it with other ingredients, without impairment of the mind. The same would no doubt be true of controlled substances such as marijuana.

The Christian approach to drugs is to use them for healing, not for recreational high or escape from our problems. When persons are suffering intense pain, the use of morphine or stronger pain relief, if necessary, is entirely appropriate and is consistent with our understanding of Proverbs 31:4–5.

The difficult judgment call comes in cases such as Prozac, Ritalin, and other drugs designed to alter one's mood. The question is whether these drugs act to restore God's natural balance in the brain, like the use of lithium to treat manic-depression, or whether they act to alter moods in a way contrary to God's intent. To calm one's nerves by restoring a natural neural imbalance is good, but to disconnect a person's natural sense of legitimate guilt would not be desirable. Nor would it be desirable for a drug to produce escape or denial, like nitrous oxide, which produces an "I don't care" attitude that is fine for undergoing an operation, but is no way to live day-to-day. These are questions that a patient needs to ask oneself in consultation with medical professionals.

The common Christian rule that is used to oppose the abuse of drugs and alcohol is that our bodies are temples of God, temples that are not to be damaged or destroyed. While this principle is indeed biblically based (1 Cor 6:19), it hinges in part on scientific judgments as to what is bad for our health, which are constantly being updated and often corrected.

The use of tobacco fits here. Tobacco is difficult to limit to amounts that do not produce a threat to one's health. A better rule to employ on the use of tobacco, the use of alcohol, the use of Valium or Oxycoton, or the overconsumption of food, is Paul's resolution, "I will not be enslaved by anything" (1 Cor 6:12). The greater the risk of addiction involved in any food, drink, or medicine we consume, the wiser we are to follow Paul's advice: I will not use any substance to which I am likely to become enslaved.

6

Common-Sense Morality

IN THE PAST TWO chapters, we have closely examined what the New Testament has to say about fornication, adultery, *aselgeia* (extreme violations of the Torah's teaching on sexuality), alcohol abuse, and *pharmakeia* (both in the senses of drug abuse and of witchcraft). To some extent, the New Testament's teachings on these subjects are more radical than the standards of the culture that surrounded the early church.

In this chapter, we will take a closer look at ethical issues where the New Testament's teachings are not quite so unique. One could easily have built a consensus in the Greco-Roman world that actions such as insulting Deity, failing to worship properly, murder, stealing, lying, greediness, and failing to treat one's neighbor as one wished oneself to be treated were all evils to some degree. Even here, however, there are plenty of questions to be answered. What exactly constitutes murder? How bad is lying, and how truthful must we be? What does Paul mean by "foul language" in Colossians 3:8? What is the difference between "blasphemy" on Jesus' sin list in Mark 7:22 (which can mean either slander against humans or blasphemy against God), and "revilers" on Paul's sin list in 1 Corinthians 6:10? What is the difference between the two terms for stealing on Paul's list in 1 Corinthians 6? How does the term "greed" function on God's sin list? And how do we use the Golden Rule, when it is so easy to jump to the mistaken conclusion that what I want is exactly how my neighbor wants to be treated?

THE GOLDEN RULE

Let's begin right here, with the Golden Rule. Jesus' words "Therefore, everything that you wish people would do to you, do so to them" (Matt 7:12) finds so many echoes from ancient Jewish and pagan writers (Hillel in

50

b. Šabb. 31a; Rabbi Aqiba in *'Abot R. Nat.* 26; Tob 4:15; *Let. Aris.* 207–8; Jerusalem Targum on Lev 19:18; Isocrates, *Nic.* 61) that some even question whether Jesus actually spoke them. We may presume that he did. The Golden Rule, in some form or other, is so commonplace in the ancient world that one might call it a piece of "common-sense morality."

The problem is that such a claim mistakenly assumes that we can all agree on what we mean by "common sense." Here is where we go wrong. We cannot assume that what we want others to do for us, is exactly what others want us to do for them. Some people love loads of fat, sugar, and salt in their food, but some people don't want to be served such food. What may be a kindness to one person may be a kick in the teeth to the next person. "I'll treat your car like it was my own" could be a scary promise if the other person's car is junk.

"Just treat everyone with common courtesy." But the rules of etiquette were not written by God, but were invented by mortal humans. They are based on cultural assumptions that change from culture to culture. Take Japan, for instance, where it is impolite to say No or to express disagreement to someone's face. Or consider how gestures that we consider friendly may be insults to those from other cultures, such as the A-OK sign in Spain or the thumbs-up sign in Australia, both of which are insults. Treating others the way we wish to be treated becomes more complicated when viewed with these pitfalls in mind.

The most deadly example of misusing the Golden Rule would be the person who assumes, "I wouldn't want to be born unwanted into a life of poverty," therefore we must abort a child who was conceived unwanted but who may want desperately to live, if he/she could speak. Jesus' words are best fulfilled when we make the same effort to understand how others wish to be treated, that we want them to make to understand us.

The problem comes whenever we assume that others share our beliefs about the right way to be treated. Here is where Joseph Fletcher's "situation ethics" theory crashes and burns. Fletcher says, "Forget moral rules. Just do the loving thing." But love cannot be left vague and undefined. God defines love for Christians by means of the very biblical teachings that Fletcher wants to throw away. "Love God and love your neighbor" is a good summary of what God wants us to do, but the rest of the New Testament's teaching spells out the details.

MURDER

We are not surprised that *phonos* (murder) appears on the New Testament sin lists, since it is a death-penalty crime in the Old Testament, and it is universally regarded as a crime by surrounding pagan cultures. But how do we define "murder"? The Hebrew verb used in the sixth commandment is *ratzach*, as opposed to the generic term *harag*, which may be used for any sort of killing, such as humans killed accidentally or in combat, or the killing of animals. The meaning of *ratzach* is more closely defined in Numbers 35, where it is clear that only killing with malicious intent qualifies as murder. The questions of whether killing in war, self-defense, or capital punishment are violations of the sixth commandment, will be left for others to pursue in depth.

But what do we do with John's statement that no murderer has eternal life within (1 John 3:15)? Perhaps we should understand that persons who have eternal life are highly unlikely to commit the crime of murder after they have come to faith. But note that John ties murder solidly to the thought crime of hatred as a natural expression thereof: "Whoever hates his brother is a murderer." We must also consider here the implications of the issue of abortion, and whether persons who have eternal life may still be capable of resorting to this act in moments of weakness. Either way, it is clear that here we have an act with tremendous potential to alienate a person from God.

Abortion is not clearly identified in Scripture as a form of murder (however, we have seen in our discussion of homosexuality how such a biblical teaching would likely be ignored even if it was explicit). Perhaps the strongest Scripture against abortion is Jesus' words in Matthew 25, "As you did (or did not do) unto the least of these, you did (or did not do) it unto me." How can we define "the least of these" so as to exclude the unborn?

The case of the accidental miscarriage in Exodus 21:22–25 is the passage that comes closest to addressing the status of the unborn, where men in a fight cause a woman to miscarry. Both the Law of Hammurabi and the Middle Assyrian Law (1100 BC) address this specific case. In Hammurabi's law, if the pregnant woman is from the noble class, the attacker shall pay ten shekels for the death of the fetus and his own daughter shall be executed if the mother dies; if the woman is a commoner, the attacker shall pay five shekels for the fetus and thirty shekels if the mother dies (CH §209–212). In the Middle Assyrian Law, the attacker is executed if he causes the death of a fetus (MAL A 50), and if a woman aborts her own fetus, she shall be impaled on a stake and left unburied (MAL A 53). In Hittite Law 17, if someone causes a woman to miscarry, the penalty is ten shekels for a full-term fetus and five shekels for a fetus in its fifth month. In the biblical passage, the husband can demand any amount the judges allow for the miscarriage, if there is no "harm." The question is whether "harm" (ʾ*asōn*, a word used elsewhere only in Genesis 42) refers to the death of the fetus or of the mother. The translators of the Greek Old Testament read this as referring to the death of the fetus, like the Middle Assyrian Law, indicating that the taking of the life of the fetus was considered an act of homicide, to be treated as a capital crime.

The rabbis declared that if a woman miscarried before the fortieth day of her pregnancy, she need not go through decontamination like one who has borne a child (*m. Nid.* 3:7). They state that for purposes of ritual cleanliness, "What is not of the form of man is not accounted [human] young" (*m. Nid.* 2:2). They also spoke to the issue of late-term abortion to save the life of the mother: "If a woman was in hard travail, the child must be cut up while it is in the womb and brought out member by member, since the life of the mother has priority over the life of the child; but if the greater part of it was already born, it may not be touched, since the claim of one life cannot override the claim of another life" (*m.* ʾ*Ohal.* 7:6).

While the rabbis are dubious about the status of the unborn child, the above quotes are all in the contexts of either miscarriage or medical emergency. The rabbis clearly opposed induced abortion.[1] The Jewish historian Josephus (*C. Ap.* 2.202) and the Jewish philosopher Philo (*Spec.* 3.108–15) also opposed induced abortion.

The pagan world was more divided in its opinion on induced abortion. Plato is famous for advocating abortion to keep women over age forty from having children (*Resp.* 5.9), as did Aristotle (*Pol.* 7.14.10). Yet there are also voices opposed to abortion in the Greco-Roman world, from Hippocrates' oath, to the first century Stoic philosopher Musonius Rufus (Discourse 15), to the Roman poet Ovid, who said, "She who first plucked forth the tender life (*fetus*) deserves to die in the warfare she began . . . Ah, women, why will you thrust and pierce with the instrument,

---

1. Gorman, *Abortion*, 45: "Jews of both regions united on the subject of deliberate abortion. Alexandrians and Palestinians of both the majority and the minority legal opinions condemned deliberate abortion as disrespect for life and as bloodshed."

and give dire poisons to your children yet unborn?" (*Am.* 2.14.5–6; 27–28). Cicero calls for capital punishment for a woman who aborted her child (*Clu.* 11.32). The second century AD Roman comic Juvenal likewise sneers at the abortionist who "takes contracts to kill humans inside the belly" (*Sat.* 6.596–97).

While the Bible itself may have been virtually silent on abortion, and while the surrounding culture was as divided on this subject as our own civilization, the early church spoke loud and clear from the get-go on the subject. As early as the *Didache*, from around the end of the first century AD, we read, "You shall not murder a child by abortion" (*Did.* 2:2). The *Epistle of Barnabas* (130 AD) repeats these exact words *(Barn.* 19:5).

The *Apocalypse of Peter* (early second century AD) pictures women who have had abortions being punished in hell by the children whom they aborted, in a pit filled to their necks with the discharge and excrement of the tortured: "These are they who have procured abortions and have ruined the work of God which he has created. Opposite them is another place where the children sit, but both alive, and they cry to God. And lightnings go forth from those children which pierce the eyes of those who, by fornication, have brought about their destruction . . . And those who slew them will be tortured forever, for God wills it to be so." (*Ethiopic Apoc. Pet.* 8, Schneemelcher edition)

Near the end of the second century AD, Athenagoras answers the charge that Christians are secret murderers by asking, "What sense does it make to think of us as murderers when we say that women who practice abortion are murderers, and will render account to God for abortion? The same man cannot regard that which is in the womb as a living being and for that reason an object of God's concern and then murder it when it has come into the light." (*Leg.* 35.6)

The Christian lawyer Tertullian (200 AD) also goes on record against abortion. He writes, "For us murder is once for all forbidden; so even the child in the womb . . . it is not lawful for us to destroy . . . To forbid birth is only quicker murder. It makes no difference whether one takes away the life once born or destroys it as it comes to birth" (*Apol.* 9.8). Clement of Alexandria (200 AD) also clearly opposes abortion (*Paed.* 2.96.1). The testimony of the early church is unanimous on this subject.

The Bible contains no prohibition of, or endorsement of, violence against one's spouse. But one may reasonably argue that if he who hates his brother is a murderer, surely he who beats his spouse is all the moreso.

Violence (against either a family member or a stranger) and murder go hand in hand; the one is a usually less-than-fatal extension of the other.

THE DESIRE FOR MORE

It is no surprise that death penalty crimes appear on the New Testament sin lists. What is mildly surprising is the appearance of *pleonexia*, greed, the desire for more. While greed is a thought crime rather than an act, Paul is the first person to equate greed with idol worship (Eph 5:5; Col 3:5). And with greed go concrete expressions of greed such as theft and swindling (*harpages*), all in a context where Paul argues against believers suing one another. We who live in a day where economic pressures push us to break every word from God (Prov 28:21: "For a piece of bread, a person will do wrong") should not be surprised that *pleonexia* and its symptoms can seriously alienate us from God.

How much is enough? Paul echoes the teaching of the Stoic philosophers when he tells the Philippians that he has learned how to be content (*autarkēs*) in all circumstances, that he has learned the secret of living with both abundance and lack (Phil 4:11–12).

The most extreme example of the simple lifestyle in the New Testament is John the Baptist. The guy who teaches us to give away our extra change of clothes (Luke 3:11) is a guy who only had one camel's hair garment and a leather belt for his wardrobe (Matt 3:4). He had no paid job, no family, no retirement account, no transportation, he ate kosher bugs and honey, and his only home was the open desert.

Like John, Jesus "has nowhere to lay his head" (Luke 9:58). He sends out his followers on tour with no money, knapsack, extra shirt, sandals, or even a stick to ward off bandits (Matt 10:9–10). He dies with only one suit of clothes.

The closest parallel to the lifestyles of Jesus and John is the simple lifestyle of the Essenes, the people who produced the Dead Sea Scrolls. Josephus describes them thus: "Riches they despise, and their community of goods is truly admirable; you will not find one among them distinguished by greater opulence than another . . . new members on admission to the sect shall confiscate [sic] their property to the order, with the result that you will nowhere see either abject poverty or inordinate wealth." (*War* 2.8.3.122) They lived a rigidly simple lifestyle, wearing only white and wearing the same clothes and shoes until they wore out (2.8.4.126). In their meals, we are told that they "are contented with the same dish day after day, loving sufficiency and rejecting great expense as harmful to mind and body." (Philo, *Hypoth.* 11.11)

Like the Essenes, the pagan Cynics lived a radical simple lifestyle. So that they would not be slaves to desire, the Cynics abstained completely from the "soft life" and its pleasures, and refused to indulge the body with even the simplest of luxuries. Most were celibate. They ate barley cakes and water, grass and watercress, instead of fish or meat or wine. They abstained from the use of hot water, beds, and even shelter, with a coarse cloak as their only covering.

Jesus and his apostles teach and model a challenging simple lifestyle. Jesus says, "Look out! Be on guard against all *pleonexia* (greed or desire for more), for life does not consist in the abundance of possessions" (Luke 12:15). We can't all live exactly like John the Baptist, unless we are willing to bring civilization to a halt and all go live off the land, while sacrificing advancements in medicine, technology, and basic utilities. We can't all practice communal living like the early church. But each of us can be inspired by their example to find ways we can imitate them. God does not demand that we give away or even sell our cabin on the lake, or our boat, or our motor home, or cutting-edge digital technology. Instead, we can ask, How can I make this item available to God to be used wherever God needs it?

STEALING

Stealing is forbidden as one of the Ten Commandments. This command does not carry a death penalty, but it is reaffirmed on several of the New Testament sin lists. Paul writes in Ephesians 4:28, "Let the thief no longer steal, but rather let them labor and work honestly with their own hands, so as to have something to share with those in need." The significance of the command against stealing is that, even though the earliest church sets an example of holding all possessions in common, God commands respect for private property.

The rabbis commanded that a thief who steals even a fraction of a cent should go all the way to Persia to pay back the person they stole from (*m. B. Qam.* 9:5). The rabbis also viewed price-gouging as a form of stealing. Some rabbis said that to charge 18 percent higher than the current market price was price-gouging, and the customer had only enough time to get a second opinion on the price before bringing their purchase back for a refund, while Rabbi Tarfon said a merchant could charge up to 33 percent above the current market price, but the customer had all day to come back and demand a refund (*m. B. Meṣiʿa* 4:3).

What is the difference between *kleptēs* (thief) and *harpax*, both of which Paul mentions in the same breath in 1 Corinthians 6:10? *Kleptō* is the standard verb for stealing used in the Septuagint's translation of the eighth commandment. *Kleptēs* is always used for a thief who sneaks or breaks in, such as where Jesus says "thieves break in and steal" (Matt 6:19–20, Luke 12:33), or where Jesus compares his coming to the surprise coming of a thief (Matt 24:43, Luke 12:39, Rev 3:3, 16:14; see also 1 Thess 5:2–4, 2 Pet 3:10).

By contrast, a *harpax* is a "snatcher" who uses force, such as an armed robber, an extortionist, or a swindler. It is the word Jesus uses for "ravenous" wolves (Matt 7:15). The term for an even more violent thief is the term *lēstēs*, which is used for Barabbas, for the thieves crucified with Jesus, the thieves in the parable of the Good Samaritan, the "danger from robbers" spoken of by Paul in his travels (2 Cor 11:26), and in Jesus' charge, "You have made it (the Temple) a den of thieves"; it is also the historian Josephus' term for anti-Roman terrorists or revolutionaries. (*Lēstēs* is not used on any of the New Testament sin lists.) *Harpax* is also used in Luke 18:11, where the Pharisee thanks God that he is not a *harpax*, and in 1 Corinthians 5:10–11, where Paul writes that one should not even associate with a *harpax* (rip-off artist?) who claims to be a Christian.

IDOLATRY

Idolatry is a capital crime in the Old Testament. Israel is the only nation in its time where it was illegal to worship other deities. Roman rule made it all but impossible for the Jews to keep all idols out of their land, although they were able to do so in Jerusalem. The question was how to avoid any sort of participation in, or support for, idolatry. Jews could not sell a Gentile anything that could be used for pagan worship; if they sold an animal that could be used in sacrifice, they had to cripple it first (*m. ʿAbod. Zar.* 1:5–6). Jews could do no business with anyone who was on their way to a pagan festival, but they could do business with those who were returning (*m. ʿAbod. Zar.* 2:3). They could do no business in towns with public idols, or in shops that were decorated with idols (*m. ʿAbod. Zar.* 1:4), although Rabbi Gamaliel used to bathe at Venus' Bathhouse (*m. ʿAbod. Zar.* 3:4). They could buy and eat flesh that was on its way to an idol's temple, but they could not eat meat that comes out of the temple (*m.* ʿ*Abod. Zar.* 2:3). If you could not be sure whether meat had been offered to an idol or not, you did not eat it; this was the issue for Christians at Corinth and at Rome. The Pharisees also never trusted a jar of wine alone with a Gentile, for fear that the Gentile might offer some of it to his or her heathen god. If in doubt, you went without wine, also. These rabbinic teachings give us a clue as to how the early church may have avoided idolatry.

The terms "blasphemers" and "revilers" both appear on Paul's sin list in 1 Corinthians 6:9–11. *Blasphēmia* can be either trashing God (which is a capital crime in the Law of Moses), or slandering fellow humans, as it is used in Romans 3:8, 1 Corinthians 10:30, and Titus 3:2. In a list such as Jesus' list in Mark 7:22, it is hard to know which meaning Jesus has in mind (or what Paul means in Eph 4:31 = Col 3:8).

The question gets even more complicated when we ask what *loidoroi* ("revilers") means as opposed to "slanderers/blasphemers." "Revile" is the word used when Jesus' enemies badmouth the man born blind in John 9:28. It is the word used in Acts 23:4 when Paul curses the high priest and is asked, "Would you revile God's high priest?" It is the word used in 1 Corinthians 4:12 when Paul says, "When reviled, we bless." Likewise, 1 Peter 2:23 says of Jesus on the cross, "When reviled, he did not counter-revile." How is this different from "slander" or "blasphemy," given that either word can be used for words spoken against either God or humans?

When we look at how both terms are used in the Greek translation of the Old Testament, we find that the verb "revile" usually means contention, strife, or quarreling, such as in Exodus 17:2, 17:7, and 21:8 (see also Num 20:3, Prov 20:3, 26:21). It is also the word used for a "contentious" spouse (Prov 25:24, 27:15). Both "revile" and "blaspheme" are used in the same sentence in 2 Maccabees 12:14, where "revile" seems to refer to abusiveness, while "blaspheme" seems to refer to saying unholy things about God. Perhaps the difference is between being contentious with God, versus attacking God's holiness. With humans, the difference appears to be between mere quarreling, and slandering a person's reputation.

USE OF LANGUAGE

Jesus has some tough words on the use of language. He says in Matthew 12:34–36, "The mouth speaks what the heart is full of . . . I tell you that on the day of judgment, you will have to give account for every careless word you utter, for by your words you will be justified, and by your words you will be condemned." When we see a politician or a comedian spewing forth constant obscenity, or even words that are "printable" but full of venom toward others, we see that the mouth speaks what the heart is full of.

The third commandment states, "You shall not take the name of the Lord your God in vain." The term "in vain" here means "for nothing." In other words, we must not use God's sacred name (or the name of Jesus, we would add) as a word to punctuate our sentences, or in any way that degrades that name or drags it through the mud. God is saying, "That's my name; don't wear it out!" To misuse God's name is what we mean by profanity. In English, the misuse of the words "damn" and "hell" as careless throwaway terms would also qualify as profanity, because these are holy subjects. Curiously, a person who does not believe in a literal future hell may use the word to blow off steam, but may be offended if you use the word properly to refer to a real final place of judgment for those who reject Christ.

So, if that is what we mean by profanity, what do we mean by "obscenity"? And on what basis do we rule out the use of obscene language that is not covered by the third commandment? Obscenity can be defined as language other than profanity that is commonly viewed as foul and/or offensive. Paul writes to the Ephesians, "Let no evil talk come out of your mouths, but only what is useful for building up, as there is need, so that your words may impart grace to those who hear" (Eph 4:29). Likewise, in the parallel passage in Colossians 3:8, Paul urges his readers to put away "filthy language" from their mouths. Finally, Paul writes to the Ephesians, "Entirely out of place is obscene, silly, and vulgar talk;[2] but instead, let there be thanksgiving" (Eph 5:4). These three relatively

---

2. The term "vulgar talk" (*eutrapelia*), found only here in the New Testament, is usually used in a positive sense elsewhere in Greek. Aristotle (*Eth. nic.* 4.8.4) says, "Those who jest with good taste are called *witty* or versatile—that is to say, full of good turns." He says in *Rhetoric* 2.12.16 that *eutrapelia* is "trained insolence" (*pepaideumenē hubris*). Paul uses this term in a negative sense.

overlooked passages are the entire biblical basis for us to avoid obscene language.

The question is, Exactly what words did Paul have in mind? It is too bad that Paul did not give us a list, and even if he had, it would have been in Greek, and I have found no such list outside the Bible of words that were considered obscene in Greek.[3] However, Old Testament Hebrew uses words that were considered obscene by later copyists. While the copyists faithfully copied the objectionable words exactly as they found them, the copyists put notes in the margin that the reader should read out loud the word *tzo'ah* ("dung") in place of the old Egyptian vulgarism *ḥ-r-'* (pronunciation uncertain), and should also read out loud the word *shakab* ("to lie with") in place of the verb *shugal* (a more vulgar term for sexual intercourse).

We have no authoritative list of English words that qualify as what Paul had in mind by "filthy talk." And everyone's personal list of what they find obscene or offensive is slightly different. Society's consensus on these words also changes over time. One standard racial slur that was not treated as obscene sixty years ago is now treated as an unprintable word to be censored from broadcasting. Likewise, there are words that are used today even in advertising that were never broadcast forty years ago, such as the expression "that sucks." (I like to ask people, "What does it suck?", which usually produces an embarrassed silence.) Indeed, I find even some of the language used in the King James translation to be unrepeatable. (See Deut 23:2, referring to illegitimate children, and 1 Sam 25:22 and similar passages, where all translations but the KJV replace the reference to urinating against a wall with the term "male".)

Scripture leaves us to exercise our own cultural sensitivity as we apply Paul's exhortation to avoid obscene language. We know that there is language that we would be wise to avoid in public conversation, because it tears down rather than building up, and because it sends the wrong message to others about our faith. We need to avoid such language, for the sake of those who hear.

---

3. Clement of Alexandria (*Paed.* 2.6.49–52) discusses obscene language. He says it is not the words, or the sexual organs, or the marriage act, that is obscene, but their unlawful use that is obscene. He also says (*Paed.* 2.9.92), "It is not wrong for us to name the organs of generation, when God is not ashamed of their function."

LYING

While the ninth commandment applies specifically only to false testimony against one's fellow human in court, the New Testament expands our understanding of this command to cover all forms of lying. (See also Lev 19:11b: "You shall not deal falsely, and you shall not lie to one another.") In Ephesians 4:25, Paul says "Therefore, putting away falsehood, let everyone speak the truth to their neighbor, for we are members of the same body." In the parallel passage in Colossians 3:9–10, we read, "Do not lie to one another, seeing that you have stripped off the old self with its practices and have clothed yourself with the new self, which is being renewed in knowledge according to the image of its creator." In John's picture of the Holy City at the end of Revelation, three times we are told that among those who will be excluded from that city will be everyone who loves and practices falsehood (21:8, 21:27, 22:15).

In the Old Testament, lies told in court are penalized only with the penalty for the crime of which the victim is falsely accused; if the liar falsely accuses someone of a capital crime, they themselves are to be executed (Deut 19:15–19). The Bible also condemns the commercial practice of lying by means of false weights and measures (Lev 19:35–36, Deut 25:13–16). Likewise, the legal rulings by the rabbis of Jesus' day about lying all deal with testimony in court and with issues of fraud in the marketplace.

Jesus raises the standard of truth to a higher level. By teaching "Let your Yes be Yes and your No be No; anything more than this comes from the evil one" (Matt 5:37), Jesus insists that the word of his followers should be more binding than an oath, like the Essenes taught.

Lying is usually an attempt to take the easy way out when telling the truth is uncomfortable. Such is the case with "little white lies." The problem is that when we are dishonest with others, people may believe our lies, which will mislead them into serving us the same terrible food again which we told them tasted so good, or buying another ugly dress like the one we told them looked so pretty, and when they find out the truth, they will be unlikely to trust our word again.

What about lying to protect someone's life, like Rahab did in Joshua 2? Some see this as the lesser of two evils. Some would argue that we are only obligated to tell the truth to someone who is not a thief or a mortal enemy who seeks our life. According to the latter view, Rahab's act was an act of pure courage, because she lied to defeat an enemy of God's people. But how does one draw the line between this kind of lying, and Oliver North lying to Congress, or politicians lying to the nation, on the grounds that the party being lied to is an enemy who does not deserve to know the truth? Or what's the difference between lying to save someone's life, and lying to protect one's job, or lying to save thousands of dollars in taxes?

OBEDIENCE TO AUTHORITY

The New Testament, Judaism, and the pagan world all shared a belief in the moral principle of obedience to authority, including parents, bosses, and government. Disobedience to parents is a death-penalty crime in the Old Testament (Exod 21:15, 17). The New Testament reaffirms this principle in Ephesians 6:1–3 and Colossians 3:20, along with a command to parents not to be harsh with their children, lest they become discouraged (Eph 6:4; Col 3:21). The Old Testament also decrees a death penalty on those who disobey the decrees of the Israelite judiciary (Deut 17:8–13).

Exodus 22:28 commands, "You shall not revile God, nor shall you curse a leader (*nasi*ʾ, "one who is lifted up," which can mean a prince, monarch, or tribal chief) of your people." Paul quotes the Septuagint translation of this verse in Acts 23:4, after unknowingly cursing the high priest. Paul's version, however, unlike the Hebrew (which uses the verb "curse"), reads, "You shall not *speak evil* of a ruler of your people." One might understand this command, as quoted by Paul, to forbid all criticism of a nation's leader. While the New Testament teaches obedience to the law of the land (even today's traffic and tax laws), and teaches respect and honor for even an emperor as wicked as Nero (Rom 13:1–8; 1 Pet 2:13–17), Exodus 22:28 only applies to pronouncing a solemn curse on a leader. It is not contrary to Scripture to identify sin or injustice in a leader, or to call that leader to repentance.

The Old Testament imposes no penalty whatsoever for slaves who disobey their masters. Slaves are urged to obey their masters in the New Testament (Eph 6:5–8; Col 3:22–25, Tit 2:9–10; 1 Pet 2:18–19), but for reasons no different than why employees should obey bosses today. No appeal is made to any inferiority or less than full human status of the slave, and masters are told to stop using threats and are warned that they too have a Master in heaven (Eph 5:9; Col 4:1).[4]

---

4. While the Bible has a few passages such as Leviticus 27 where different "valua-

While much of the New Testament's moral teaching can be found in some form in the surrounding Jewish and Greco-Roman cultures of the first century AD, as we have seen in this chapter, the New Testament does not plagiarize or parrot the teachings of the surrounding culture. One could rather argue that the moral teaching on which they all agree is simply evidence that they are all responding to the same voice of conscience. In some cases, the New Testament improves upon the pagan ethic, lifting it to a higher level.

God has a list of sins, a list we did not invent, a list that has been revealed within the hearts of those who have ears to hear. But God has not spoken clearly or definitively on every moral subject that we humans are concerned about. In our next chapter, we'll take a look at those moral issues on which God has not issued an opinion that would give us grounds to say, "Thus says the Lord."

---

tions" are attached to men and women, young and old, the Bible never sanctions lower status for any of these classes of people, any more than we are lower status than today's baseball player who is "worth" (= paid) $10 million per year. Indeed, in the Leviticus passage, women, children, and the elderly are given "discounts" on the amount that must be paid for them to fulfill a vow.

7

What's *Not* on God's Sin List?

THE URBAN LEGEND GOES that W. C. Fields was seen reading the Bible. When asked why he was doing so, Fields is said to have replied, "I'm looking for loopholes."

Have you ever tried to make a list of rules for your home or office (or even write laws for your community) that will cover every possible kind of mischief, without any loopholes? It's almost impossible. The best you can do is to make a list of clearly forbidden behaviors that can serve as examples of other undesired behaviors that there wasn't room to list.

God has not given us a comprehensive list of sins in the Bible. Just because a behavior is not named as a sin in the Bible does not mean that this behavior is pleasing to God. As we saw in the case of alcohol, the fact that God says through the apostle, "Do not be drunk with wine," does not mean it's okay to get drunk with beer, whiskey, marijuana, or cocaine. In this case, wine serves as a representative example of substance abuse. The Bible may only name incest and bestiality out of all the abnormal behaviors on the American Psychological Association's DSM-IV list, but that does not mean that God approves the rest of what is on the APA's list of abnormal behaviors. The Bible does not explicitly condemn either nudity or cannibalism (other than that human flesh is not kosher), but that does not mean these are not evil. But when neither the behavior in question, nor any similar behavior, is named as a sin anywhere in Scripture, and yet we know that the behavior was well-known to the people to whom Scripture was first written, then we do well to consider whether this behavior is a top priority offense with God.

GAMBLING

Gambling is one example of a vice that was well-known in biblical times, but is virtually never identified as sin in Scripture or by early believers. In the Old Testament, the only two reported instances of gambling are where Samson makes (and loses) a bet with his groomsmen (Judg 14:11–18), and where an officer of the Assyrian king makes a bet with King Hezekiah of Judah, "I will give you two thousand horses, if you are able on your part to set riders on them" (2 Kgs 18:23). Otherwise, gambling first appears on the radar screen of the biblical world during Greco-Roman times. In the lone New Testament account commonly cited as an instance of gambling, the dividing of Jesus' clothes (found in all four Gospels), one may question whether the instance even qualifies as an example of gambling. The actual language used by the Gospel writers refers to the casting of "lots," and there is no evidence that the soldiers were risking any money or possessions.

According to one Greek myth, Poseidon, Zeus, and Hades divided the world in a dice game. In another such myth, Mercury wins a dice game with the Moon and collects 1/70 of her light as winnings (Plutarch, *Is. Os.* 12.3.355 D-E).

In the fifth century BC, the Greek historian Xenophon tells the story of how Queen Parysatis of Persia avenges the murder of her son by winning possession of the slave who killed him in a dice game (*Life of Artaxerxes* 17:3–10). Aristotle lumps gamblers together with thieves and robbers: both "are to be classed as mean, as showing sordid greed (*aischrokerdeis*) . . . the dicer making gain out of his friends, to whom one ought to give; hence both are guilty of sordid greed (*aischrokerdeis*), trying as they do to get gain from wrong sources " (*Eth. nic.* 4.1.43). The Athenian orator Callistratus refers to dice-players who, "if they win one success, throw for double stakes," noting that "the majority of such people become utterly impoverished" (Xenophon, *Hell.* 6.3.16).

The Roman historian Tacitus describes Germans in his day betting all they had on dice games, even their freedom:

> What is extraordinary, they play at dice, when sober, as a serious business; and that with such a desperate venture of gain or loss, that, when everything else is gone, they set their liberties and persons on the last throw. The loser goes into voluntary servitude; and, though the youngest and strongest, patiently suffers himself to be bound and sold. Such is their obstinacy in a bad

practice — they themselves call it honor. The slaves thus acquired are exchanged away in commerce, that the winner may get rid of the scandal of his victory . . .[1]

The Roman historian Suetonius describes the gambling habits of several Roman emperors. He writes, "Augustus did not mind being called a gambler; he diced openly, in his old age, too, simply because he loved the game." (*Lives of the Caesars* 2.71, Penguin) In the same passage, Suetonius quotes three letters where Augustus tells about his gambling, including one where he tells of losing 200 gold pieces during the festival of Minerva, and another where he tells of giving money to each of his dinner guests "in case they feel like dicing or playing 'odd and even' at table." Suetonius states that Nero "would stake 4,000 gold pieces on each pip of the winning throw at dice" (6.30).

About the emperor Claudius, Suetonius writes (5.33), "So fervent was his devotion to dice that he published a book on the subject, and used to play, while out driving, on a special board fitted to his carriage which kept the game from upsetting." The philosopher Seneca ridiculed Claudius for his gambling habit. He pictured the departed emperor in Hades condemned to pick up dice forever, putting them in a box without a bottom (*The Pumpkinification of Claudius* 15.1–2).

Juvenal, the Roman comedian, complains around 100 AD, "When did gambling arouse such passion? People now come to try their luck at the gaming table not with their wallets but betting from a treasure chest . . . Is it not pure madness to lose a hundred thousand sesterces and yet grudge a shirt to a shivering slave?" (*Sat.* 1:88–93) Steinmetz states that "at the epoch when Constantine abandoned Rome never to return, every inhabitant of that city, down to the populace, was addicted to gambling."[2]

Romans both frowned on and yet admired gambling, because the willingness to place huge bets was viewed by some as a sign of bravery. Cicero viewed gambling as superstition; he despised it as an attempt to force the hand of the gods (*Div.* 2). Gambling was prohibited starting with the *Lex alearia* law (204 BC), except during the Feast of Saturnalia, although the offense was widely ignored as long as it was done in private.[3] Heavy betting took place at chariot races, which was permitted

---

1. Tacitus, "Germany," §24, lines 5–12.

2. Steinmetz, *Gaming Table*, 1:68.

3. Cicero (*Philippic* 2.23.56) complained that one convicted gambler "would not

by the *Lex Titia de aleatoribus,* which allowed betting on sports that involved bravery on the part of competitors. Gamblers often employed self-denial, incantations, and fortune-tellers to invoke the favor of the gods in advance. The rabbis of Jesus' day lumped "dice-players" together with unsavory characters such as loan-sharks, pigeon-flyers, and traffickers in seventh-year produce, all of whom were disqualified to be witnesses or jurors in court (*m. Sanh.* 3:3).

Laws were passed to limit gambling losses. According to the *Lex Cornelia* law on gambling passed in 81 BC, creditors could not sue for gambling debts, but losers could sue for losses, which were treated like stolen property. One of the issues about gambling in Roman law, according to the Roman legal scholar Ulpian, is that sometimes persons were forced into playing against their will, which was viewed as a form of robbery. The offender could be sentenced to the quarries or to imprisonment in chains.[4]

The only early Christian opinion in favor of gambling has been found on the back of a game set, where an inscription reads, "If after this manner one should play at the *alveus* [a dice-like game piece], Jesus Christ gives victory, and assistance to those who wrote his name, even in such trifling matters as playing this game."[5] It is unclear whether the writer of this inscription played for money.

The only early Christian writers to criticize gambling were Clement of Alexandria, Tertullian, and Pseudo-Cyprian (*De aleatoribus,* "About Dice-players," described as our earliest Christian sermon in Latin), all from the early third century AD. Clement of Alexandria writes, "The game of dice is to be prohibited, and the pursuit of gain, especially by dicing, which many keenly follow. Such things the prodigality of luxury invents for the idle. For the cause is idleness, and a love for frivolities apart from the truth" (*Paed.* 3.11.75). Tertullian says Christians should not play dice because "frenzy (Latin *furor*) is forbidden us" (*Spect.* 16). Tertullian is also widely quoted as saying, "If you say that you are a Christian when you are a dice-player, you say you are what you are not, because you are a partner with the world," but this quote is now found to be from *De aleatoribus* 8, a document full of scathing rebuke toward Christians who gamble (see translation in appendix 3).

---

even shrink from gambling in the Forum."

4. Scott, *Civil Law,* 82–83.

5. Schwartz, *Bones,* 33.

It appears that gambling was not a part of the normal experience of early believers until we first begin to hear them object to it. Clement's and Tertullian's objections are not from Scripture, and are based on different rationales: that it is either a product of laziness (Clement), or it is too much excitement (Tertullian), neither of which can be drawn clearly from Scripture.

By the time of *De aleatoribus*, what's going on in the mainstream of the Roman world has finally invaded the Church (even though Christianity is still an underground illegal movement), and the anonymous author of this document breathes fire and venom against the practice as being totally incompatible with Christian faith. Pseudo-Cyprian argues that dice-playing is idolatrous, it is closely associated in practice with other evils such as theft and prostitution, it is an obsession/addiction, and it involves the waste of scandalous amounts of money (see appendix 3).

In light of all this evidence, the Bible's silence on the morality of gambling is particularly striking. In fact, with so little basis to condemn it, it is surprising how strong the almost universal taboo against gambling proved to be in Western civilization, and how long it lasted.

None of this means that gambling is good. Gambling may be viewed as a waste of money, one that often victimizes poor people who cannot afford to lose it. Gambling may be classed as a form of get-rich-quick scheme that Proverbs 13:11 frowns upon ("Wealth hastily gotten will dwindle, but whoever gathers little by little will increase it"). It may be rightly described as a form of stealing from those who play, and/or as poor management of God's money. For many, gambling is an addiction, to which Paul would say, "I will not be enslaved by anything" (1 Cor 6:12). But if gambling were a major issue with God, God would probably have addressed the issue in Scripture, seeing how prevalent the practice was in the biblical world.

OTHER MODERN VICES NOT MENTIONED IN SCRIPTURE

There are numerous modern vices that may be displeasing to God, but are never clearly presented in Scripture as moral imperatives to avoid. For instance, the use of steroids by athletes is treated as if it were carved in stone on Mount Sinai. We saw baseball players such as Mark McGwire get vilified when they confessed to steroid use. But does God really care about the use of steroids? Which of God's commands does it violate, other than in cases where athletes have lied to cover it up? One could argue that steroids are a form of cheating, but it is only cheating against rules that were made up by mortal humans.

Another example would be torture. Let me clearly state that we all find the basic notion of torture to be morally repugnant. However, the Bible is absolutely silent about torture. There is neither clear endorsement nor clear condemnation, and yet we know that torture was widely known and practiced throughout the biblical period. The Bible has no explicit teaching against torture. In fact, when Jesus confronts the Legion of demons, they cry, "Have you come to torture (*basanisai*) us before the time? (Matt 8:29) I beg you by God, do not torment me (*basanises*— Mark 5:7, Luke 8:28)!" Jesus has nothing bad to say against the torturers in the parable of the Unforgiving Servant; in fact, Jesus seems to accept torture here as a fact of life (Matt 18:34). In the Revelation of Jesus Christ to John, the devil and his accomplices will be tortured (*basanisthesontai*) day and night forever and ever (Rev 20:10), presumably by agents of God. About the only biblical hint that torture might be bad is the fact that examining a prisoner by scourging is forbidden when the prisoner is a Roman citizen (Acts 20:24–29).

One may respond that torture violates the Golden Rule, the imperative that we must treat others the way that we wish to be treated. While this is a valid point, the Golden Rule is not clear enough to be used as proof that torture is evil enough to be considered a crime against the image of God. The Golden Rule only works when how we wish to be treated matches up to how others wish to be treated, and we know that these two sets of expectations vary wildly from person to person, and from culture to culture. There is also the problem of how to define torture: where do we draw the line between dehumanizing treatment, and mere intimidation or harassment? Christians do well to oppose the use of torture, if not to ban it entirely, but we must be careful not to be adamantly dogmatic about a practice about which the Bible is completely silent in an age where it was widely known and practiced.

Another case of an action not forbidden in Scripture (for which the technology did not exist in biblical times) is the case of sex-change operations. The Law of Moses excludes those who have had their male organ cut off from entering the house of God, but Isaiah 56 and the New Testament clearly open the kingdom of God to eunuchs. While the person who has a sex-change operation may violate no binding command of God by so doing, this does not mean that their choice is good. While such a person may have replaced their original genital organs with a different set of organs, such an action does not change who they are. Every other cell in their body remains the original gender that God created them, and the person must take anti-rejection drugs to prevent their body from rejecting the organs that they have transplanted into their body, and while the transplanted organs may be alive, whether they can function as they were created to function remains open to question. The man who receives the organs of a woman is still a man, and if he has intercourse with a man, even if the right parts are there, it is still arguably a male-to-male act of intercourse. While this act of surgically changing one's gender is not explicitly forbidden in Scripture, it can hardly be good in the eyes of God, and is arguably a rejection of the Creator's good gift.

DEFINING JUSTICE

The Bible condemns injustice, but rarely does the Bible give specific examples that we can apply dogmatically today. We may agree that farm workers are poorly paid, but what exactly would be a fair wage for them? God has not specified what a minimum wage or a fair price should be. This does not excuse Christians from the necessity of making our best guess with the help of God and our conscience as we seek to treat others with justice in the marketplace. But it should restrain us from pronouncing judgment in the name of God on questions of justice where God has not spoken.

The same is true for the related concept of oppressing the poor. While God clearly and regularly condemns the oppression of the poor, the Bible does not clearly define what oppression looks like in terms that resemble the practices for which this claim is invoked today.

The same is true for our entire modern category of human rights. Proverbs 29:7 says, "A righteous person knows the rights of the poor; a wicked person does not understand such knowledge." Unfortunately, because these rights were clearly understood by God's people at the time, God did not spell them out in writing for us. [6]

Is health care, for instance, a human right? It would be difficult to tell that to an apostle like Paul who did not treat even food as a human

---

6. And even if God did spell out these rights, would we be willing to accept what God said to people in the Late Bronze Age? Or would we dismiss what God said to them on the grounds that times have changed?

right, judging from his advice to a church plagued with freeloaders: "If anyone will not work, let them not eat" (2 Thess 3:10). On the other hand, John asks, "How does God's love abide in anyone who has the world's goods and sees their brother/sister in need, yet refuses to help?" (1 John 3:17) It would be better to describe health care as an imperative of compassion than to call it a human right.

Each of us has our own private list of behaviors where we draw the line of unacceptability, behaviors that we consider to be totally unacceptable for Christians and particularly for our leaders. It is only sensible and fair to take our unspoken lists and make them explicit. Instead of the "fidelity and chastity" clause in the Presbyterian Church (USA)'s Book of Order, the church might have done better to spell out a brief, specific code of ethics containing more than just sexual ethics.

Our moral felony lists do vary from person to person, but most of them tend to include adultery, substance abuse, domestic violence, and embezzlement. We already have a consensus on what sins present a danger to the individual who continues to practice them, and to the Christian community that tolerates them. We need to build consensus on our lists wherever possible. Our current moral debate centers on whether *porneia* and homosexual sex also belong in that consensus.

Where God has not clearly spoken, we should beware of putting words in God's mouth. But where God has spoken to a world where the situation was comparable to ours, we must not dismiss what God has said.

8

The Sky's the Limit

IMAGINE A VIDEO GAME where, no matter how well you do or how high you score, there are higher and higher levels that require ever-increasing speed and skill, to where eventually, it is never humanly possibly to win. That's the scenario God presents to those who think they can be good enough to reach God by obedience to the laws we have been discussing so far.

In the story of the Rich Young Ruler (Matt 19:16–22 = Mark 10:17–22, Luke 18:18–23), Jesus meets a man who wants to know, "Teacher, what good deed must I do to have eternal life?" Jesus tells him, "If you wish to enter into life, keep the commandments," and proceeds to highlight the Ten Commandments and "You shall love your neighbor as yourself." The young man claims, "All of these I have kept since my youth. What do I still lack?" Jesus looks at the young man with love and says, "If you would be perfect, go, sell your possessions and give to the poor, and come, follow me." The young man goes away sadly, because he had "many possessions."

Jesus goes on to emphasize that it is next to impossible for a person with great wealth, like this young man, to reach God on their own. Does wealth itself disqualify a person from heaven? No. Zacchaeus does not give away all that he has (Luke 19:8–9). There are wealthy heroes of faith all over the Bible, from Abraham to Job to the women who provided for Jesus and his followers in Luke 8:1–3. The issue in the case of the Rich Young Ruler was: "if you would be perfect."

Jesus says, "Unless your righteousness exceeds that of the scribes and Pharisees, you will never enter the kingdom of heaven" (Matt 5:20). The Pharisees had high standards: obey the 623 commands in the Law of Moses, plus the 800 pages of rules they added to that Law. Jesus puts the bar even higher! Jesus puts the bar sky-high, if we would try to reach God by obedience to God's law.

Jesus' brother James says the same thing. He writes, "Whosoever would obey the whole Law and offend in one point, has become guilty of it all" (Jas 2:10). James never uses the term "commandments" in the plural. He views the commandment of God as a unit. It doesn't matter which provision of God's law you have violated; it is all one law. All it takes is one violation to make you a lawbreaker.

If we go beyond the biblical sin lists to passages such as the Sermon on the Mount (Matt 5–7), the Greatest Commandment (Deut 6:4), the Love Commandment (John 13:34), the Sheep and the Goats (Matt 25:31–46), and Paul's definition of love in 1 Corinthians 13, we will find just how impossibly high God has set the bar for those who seek to be saved by their own goodness.

Take, for example, the Greatest Commandment: "You shall love the Lord your God with *all* your heart, with *all* your soul, and with *all* your might." Who can honestly claim to always love God wholeheartedly? Or take Jesus' command, "Love one another, as I have loved you." How can we possibly equal the self-sacrificial love that Jesus has shown to us? As Paul points out in Romans 5, it's hard to enough to find someone who is willing to give their life for a good person (let alone a kidney for a stranger, we might add), but Christ gave his life for us while we were still God's enemies. If our salvation depends on how well we obey these two priority commands from God, we are toast.

Or take the parable of the Sheep and the Goats, where Jesus says the nations of the world will be judged by how they have treated him through how they have treated the "least of these." This is a popular passage for those who reject the teaching of salvation through Christ alone. But taken by itself, this passage becomes a message of salvation by our own good deeds. This is Good News?? And how much is enough? To be brutally honest, how often have we failed to do unto Christ by what we have failed to do for the least of these?

If God judges us by how well we love one another, what does that look like? The answer may be found in 1 Corinthians 13:4–8: "Love is patient, love is kind. It is not jealous, it does not brag, it is not conceited, it does not behave shamefully, it does not seek its own way. It is not easily provoked, it does not keep a record of wrongs, it does not rejoice over wrongdoing, but rejoices in the truth. Love bears all things, always has faith, always hopes, always endures. Love never fails (literally: falls)." Who can honestly say, "That's me. That's how I live. That's how I treat everyone"?

Or let's look at Jesus' teachings in the Sermon on the Mount: "Whoever is angry with one's brother/sister shall be in danger of the judgment, whoever says *Rēqa'* (Empty-head) to one's brother/sister shall be liable to the (Jewish) Supreme Court, and whoever says *Moron!* will be subject to the Gehenna of fire" (Matt 5:22). Or what about Jesus' teaching in 5:39 not to retaliate or resist one who is evil? Or his teachings to give to the one who asks from you (anyone? everyone?—Matt 5:42), or to love our enemies (Matt 5:44)? Jesus wraps up this part of the sermon with the line, "Be perfect, even as your heavenly Father is perfect" (Matt 5:48).

Or take the chapter that is possibly the most challenging passage in the Old Testament: Job 31. As Job makes his final protest of his innocence, he claims that he has never looked with desire upon a virgin (31:1), nor has his heart been enticed by a married woman (31:9). He says he has not practiced deceit or falsehood (31:5), nor rejected any complaint from his servants (31:13), nor withheld anything the poor desired (31:16), nor has he failed to share his meals with the poor (31:17) or left them without clothes to wear (31:19–20), nor taken advantage of them (31:21), and he has always taken in travelers and strangers in need of lodging (31:32). Job claims that he has never trusted in or taken delight in his wealth (31:24-25), or rejoiced at the ruin of those who hate him (31:29), or wished that they would die (31:30). He even says that he has never mistreated his land (31:38–40). As I look at Job's ethic, all I can do is say, "Woe is me, if this is the standard God sets for all of us!"

Jesus and his apostles give us a sky-high ethic, one that it is no more possible to live by, than it is possible to walk on one foot for a lifetime without outside support. The act is not humanly impossible, but it is impossible to live that way consistently for a lifetime. One can argue that Jesus is only giving us ideals, rather than commands that must never be broken on penalty of judgment. But anyone who seeks to reach God by their own goodness or obedience to God's commands must reckon with Jesus' teachings as evidence that they are far from the perfection that God requires.

As we have examined God's sin list, we have seen that even without the commands that God only intended for Israel, there is too much to obey, if obedience is the way to be saved. If we see God's law as advice to help us avoid needless heartache, we can see that life is so full of pitfalls, it's a wonder that sin has not made us more miserable than we already are. If we see God's law as an expression of what God loves and hates, we may get the impression that God is totally exasperated with us. If we are fearful or miserable at this point in our study, we need to reexamine our understanding of our relationship with God. There is Good News that can totally change our perspective on God's law.

9

Good News for Those Who Fail

IF YOU HAD TOLD me thirty years ago that I would be writing an entire book on God's list of sins, I would never have believed it. I wouldn't have wanted to. You see, going back ten years further, into my early teen years, the law of God was a burden to me from which I would have been glad to be delivered, if only I had known how.

Don't get me wrong. I was no juvenile delinquent: no sex, drugs, or trouble with the police. I had no obvious reason to believe I was going to hell. I even had within me a desire to be right with God. So when I was confirmed into membership in my local church, I made a sort of "New Year's resolution" to God to be the best person I could possibly be, and hoped that my good deeds would outweigh my bad deeds in the end.

The trouble is, I had a conscience that was too honest to believe that I was being good enough. Perhaps I was not literally committing idolatry, murder, or adultery, but I knew that I broke these laws in my heart. And I knew that God expected us, not only not to do evil, but also to do good. But I could never know if I had done enough. I knew that Jesus died for our sins, but I couldn't figure out how that applied to me, how I could know that I was worthy enough for him to save me. I had no idea how a person could know that they have been put right with God. I didn't think that anyone else knew, either.

But when I got into high school, I found that there were people who knew that they were saved. They had the assurance that they had eternal life, the very assurance that I wished I had. One of these persons was our new assistant pastor, who took our youth group to hear other young people who had found Christ (this was in the days of the Jesus Movement of the 1970s). After a year of searching for what so many other people had found, I went to my pastor on the first night of a youth group trip to Arkansas and asked him to help me find the assurance I was looking for.

"Jim," I said, "I have been trying hard to be a good person, but I don't know if I've been good enough. How can I know that I've done enough to be saved?"

Jim responded by quoting Ephesians 2:8–9, a passage I had never heard before: "For it is by grace that you have been saved, through faith, and that is not of yourselves, it is the gift of God, not by works, lest anyone should boast." Then Jim explained what the word grace means. He said it means: undeserved favor.

"Jim!" I said. "Are you trying to tell me that salvation is free? Are you trying to tell me that it's a free gift, a gift we can't earn or deserve?" He said yes. "Jim," I said, "that goes against everything I ever heard in church!"

Could it be? Hadn't I always heard, "Be a good person, and you'll go to heaven"? How could this news be true? How could God give salvation as a free gift? If that was true, what was there to keep everyone from accepting this free gift? But the more I thought about what Jim said, the more I realized that this was the missing part of the puzzle that I had been searching for: salvation, not by my own goodness, but through a gift from God that I could never earn or deserve. All I could do was accept it in faith. Now I understood that what Jesus did was enough to put me right with God and give me the assurance of eternal life, not based on how much I had done, but based totally on Jesus and what he did for me. That night I prayed to receive this gift of God, and God gave me the assurance of eternal life.

Throughout my high school and college years, I resisted any teaching or Bible verse that appeared to question, or required us to add anything to, the grace of God. For me, like for Martin Luther, the message of God's grace in Romans and Galatians was the heart of the Gospel, and I viewed James's line "faith without works is dead" as a threat to my assurance of salvation. Whenever I heard people who had been saved out of a life of terrible sin preach that we need to repent of sin or make Jesus our Lord, I used to think, No! We can never completely repent of everything we do wrong, and we can never completely make Jesus our Lord, because we will always continue to sin.

It has only been in recent years that I have come to understand why those who had come to Christ out of a life of terrible sin would insist that we must repent or make Jesus our Lord before we can be saved. They were speaking from their experience. They'd had sin in their lives that they had refused to give up that stood in the way of them following Jesus, sin that I would never have dreamed that God would tolerate in the life of a Christian.

As the debate about sin has progressed in our culture, and particularly within our churches, as large numbers have argued that unrepentant fornication and homosexual behavior are OK with God, I find myself saying the same thing I used to resist when I heard it from newly saved hippies in the 1970s: A person who wishes to be saved must be willing to repent or turn from sin. Faith without works is dead. A person who says, "I know him," and does not do what Jesus says, is a liar, and the truth is not in him/her. We cannot say, "Jesus is Lord," while continuing to practice fornication, cohabitation, the gay lifestyle, drug abuse, domestic violence, embezzlement, or any other unrepentant sin. I never thought I would become a spokesperson for the necessity of the Law of God. But that's how I have come to write this book.

For those who wonder, "Has God really spoken?" on the issues we have discussed on God's sin list, the purpose of this book is to clarify, to help you find answers on the questions being asked today about what is sin. But if this study of what is sin has created burdens of guilt and fear for you, the problem may be a misunderstanding of God's law, or an unawareness of God's grace. The Good News is: none of us can earn or deserve the mercy of God. Having taken a look together at all the ways that we can and do fall short of what God has a right to expect from us, we can certainly see why! None of us can possibly do it all without sinning again and again and again.

That's why there is no way we can add any requirement or good deed to God's free gift of salvation. Even faith is not an add-on; not only does faith come from God rather than from us (remember Eph 2:8!), but faith is no more of a meritorious act than the action of a drowning person who grabs the rescue rope. We are not saved by faith plus our own goodness; we are saved by God's free gift, period!

Where do good works come in, then? They are a response of gratitude. They are evidence that our faith is real. A person who receives the undeserved mercy of God will want to live in a way that says "Thank you!" That does not mean they get rid of sin in their life all at once. But it does mean they get a new heart that loves God and loves God's word, and wants to get rid of sin. If you see these signs of God at work in your life, that is good news indeed.

If the love of Christ has taken control of your life, you will want to do what pleases God, and avoid what grieves the heart of God. But how do we know what pleases or grieves God? That's where knowing the law of God comes in, which is another purpose of this book. God's law is an expression of the heart and character of God. As we long to grow in our relationship with our Beloved, we need to know more about what God loves, and what God wants us to turn away from.

Even here, however, we need to beware of forgetting that our relationship with God is based, not on our performance, not on how good we are, but on the grace of God. If our relationship with God is based on our performance, we'll either be always walking on eggshells around God, or else we'll be constantly feeling less than joyful around God, feeling like God is always finding fault with us. We need to truly believe that God's love for us has always been, and will always be, free, undeserved, and unconditional. Believing in God's grace toward us can set us free to treat others with the same unconditional love. If we do good, we can't boast about it; it's God working in us. If we fail, God never loved us because we were good, anyway.

God's sin list was never intended to show us how we can earn our way to God. Nor was it ever intended to leave us permanently condemned and hopeless. It was designed to show us how badly we need the salvation that only Christ can give us, to drive us into his arms. If you have found and received his mercy, God's sin list is there to be a guide to avoid the pitfalls of needless heartache on this side of heaven. Thanks be to God that God has not left us clueless, but has given us guidance through Jesus and his apostles on how to live in the light of his wonderful free gift of mercy that we call grace.

Appendix 1

The Meaning of "Cut Off from One's People"

THE PREDOMINANT POSITION ON the meaning of the penalty "cut off from one's people" at the moment (known in Judaism as the *kareth* penalty) is the one developed by rabbinic Judaism, that "cut off from one's people" is a penalty imposed by God, consisting of premature death of the offender and/or the extinction of the offender's descendants. This interpretation goes back at least as far as the Septuagint, where the Hebrew term *karath* as a penalty is consistently translated into Greek by terms such as "exterminate" or "destroy." However, we can also trace a different tradition of interpretation, beginning with Ezra's post-exilic community and continuing to the community at Qumran. For instance, the language used by the Targums (paraphrases of the Bible in Aramaic) when they translate this word sounds more like expulsion than extermination. The Jewish Targums always use the Aramaic term "to cause to go out" to translate this penalty. The Samaritan Targum uses two terms to translate this penalty, one that means "to cut or break off," and one that means "to be uprooted, detached, or removed".

Both Philo and Josephus see this penalty as meaning death. Yet Josephus also tells us that a different interpretation also existed in practice during Maccabean times: "And whenever anyone was accused by the people of Jerusalem of eating unclean food or violating the Sabbath or committing any other such sin, he would flee to the Shechemites, saying that he had been unjustly expelled." (*Ant.* 11.8.7)

Qumran uses the verb *karath* to describe the final annihilation of the wicked. Yet Qumran also gives more evidence for the use of punitive expulsion than any other Jewish source, although it uses verbs other than *karath* for this penalty. Qumran states that one "who transgresses a word of the Torah of Moses deliberately or through negligence, shall be banished from the Council of the Community and never come back again." (1QS VIII 22–23) Here we see how Qumran implements the penalty for "sinning with a high hand" in Numbers 15:30–31. Qumran may be giving us the Sadducean understanding of *karath*.

Josephus also describes such expulsions from what is presumably the Qumran community: "Men convicted of major offenses are expelled from the order, and the outcast often comes to a most miserable end; for bound as he is by oaths and customs he cannot share the diet of non-members, so is forced to eat grass till his starved body wastes away and he dies." (*War* 2.8.8)

The Mishnah discusses thirty-six *kareth* offenses and their punishments in tractate *Kerithot*. If these offenses were committed unintentionally, the Mishnah prescribes a sin offering. But in *m. Mak.* 3:2, several of these crimes are penalized by scourging. The chapter goes on to state that if an offender is scourged, the penalty of "extermination" no longer applies, since justice has been satisfied. The Mishnah reflects the standard "extermination" tradition of the rabbis found throughout the Talmud.

The problem with the consensus developed by rabbinic Judaism is that the history of early Jewish interpretation does not guarantee reliable results, especially when dealing with social or cultural elements that may have been lost to later memory. The history of interpretation of the command "You shall not boil a kid in its mother's milk" is proof of the unreliability of using the history of interpretation to determine original meaning.

Von Rad is possibly the first modern scholar to argue that the *kareth* penalty refers to "the excommunication of the offender," although he does not offer any evidence to substantiate his theory.[1] Von Rad's theory has been followed by Westermann, Pope, Elliger, Levine, and Zimmerli.[2] But few have offered any evidence for this theory.

The only extensive attempt to examine the *kareth* penalty discovered so far is the 1978 dissertation of Donald Wold. Wold argues that the phrase "cut off from one's people" is a divine extermination curse, a parallel to standard Near Eastern curses that call on a deity to "erase one's name and seed from the land." Wold interprets the term *'amim* to

---

1. Von Rad, *Theology*, 1:264–68.

2. Westermann, *Genesis*, 266–67; Pope, "Excommunication," 184; Elliger, *Leviticus*, 101; Levine, *Leviticus*, 242; Zimmerli, "Eigenart," 1–26.

mean one's family or kin. He argues that to be "cut off" from one's kin not only means eternal isolation after death, but also the extermination of one's family line. Wold sees the witness of ancient Judaism as being unanimous in support of this position. Wold rejects the punitive expulsion theory. So does Jacob Milgrom, his doctoral advisor.[3] Sophie Lafont is possibly the only scholar to connect the possibility of banishment in Israel with evidence for banishment in the ancient Near East.[4] My dissertation seeks to expand the evidence identified by Lafont and by Raymond Westbrook (see bibliography).

Some brief observations on the question, Can *karath* be used to mean punitive expulsion? Outside of Hebrew, the *krt* root is only used to denote physical cutting. It is not used for either of the two chief secondary meanings it has developed in Hebrew: removal and destruction. These two secondary meanings account for 149 out of the 288 times that the verb is used in the Hebrew Bible.

The basic meaning of *karath* is to "cut, sever, or separate." Spatial separation from a specific place is the meaning of *karath* in Joshua 3:16, where the waters of the Jordan are "cut off." One key example of this usage is 1 Kings 9:7, where YHWH promises that if the nation disobeys, "I will cut off Israel from the land that I have given them." The fulfillment of this promise becomes the ultimate example of banishment, the Exile. In the parallel to this passage (2 Chr 7:20), *natash* is used for *karath*, clearly demonstrating a non-fatal meaning for *karath* in this case.

In all cases of the "cut off penalty," the verb *karath* means "removal." In a few narrowly defined cases, it refers to an extreme form of removal (death), such as in the case of breaking the Sabbath in Exodus 31:14, where both penalties are declared. Otherwise, "expulsion" makes the best sense. The passages where *kareth* appears most likely to be punitive expulsion are the passages that meet the following criteria: 1. There is a *min*-clause that clearly delineates a community from which the subject is separated; 2. ʿ*am* is either used in the singular or has been replaced by "Israel," "the congregation," or "from my presence"; 3. No contextual obstacles exist to a meaning of expulsion rather than death. 4. The verb is in the nipʿal conjugation, which is less likely to connote destruction than the hipʿil conjugation.

3. Milgrom, *Leviticus*, 457–60.

4. Lafont, *Femmes*, 184–85.

The shortage of evidence for the expulsion penalty would appear to be an argument against the theory advocated here. There is only one statute found so far in any Near Eastern law code that explicitly calls for this practice. However, Westbrook cautions that Near Eastern law codes are not comprehensive legislation, and that we must therefore beware of "arguments from silence."[5] Furthermore, both Finkelstein and Loewenstamm point out that there is very little textual evidence that penalties in any of the Near Eastern law codes were carried out as stipulated.[6] For example, virtually no executions for adultery or murder are recorded, other than the use of the river ordeal at Mari, although there are numerous instances of blood money being paid. Evidence for actual legal practice must be sought in texts outside the ancient law codes, such as royal decrees, court records, historical texts, and letters, which is what we have to do in Egypt, from which we have no written laws.

Criteria must be delineated for what qualifies as punitive expulsion. First, fugitives from justice or fugitives from capture will be eliminated from consideration in this study. Second, peoples who have been exiled as a result of conquest will not be included; an identifiable crime must be the reason for the expulsion. Third, other expulsions that are non-judicial in nature will not be included, such as evictions from a house or a field. Finally, punitive expulsion will be defined to include not only expulsion from a city or nation, but also banishment from temple or palace.

We begin with the second millennium BC and earlier. The only statute that calls for punitive expulsion is Law §154 from the Code of Hammurabi: "If a gentleman has had intercourse with his daughter, they shall make that gentleman leave the city." From an earlier period comes the myth of Enlil and Ninlil, where the chief god of the Sumerian pantheon is banished as an *uzug* (sex-criminal or unclean person) for the crime of impregnating an underage female. The practice of banishing such an "unclean person" is also found on Gudea Statue B and on Cylinder B (around 2100 BC). Also, in the myth of Nergal and Ereškigal, the goddess Ereškigal claims that she cannot perform her duties as a deity because she has been defiled by illicit intercourse (the term used here is the Akkadian cognate of *uzug*—she says, "I am unclean—I can-

---

5. Westbrook, *Studies*, 5–7.

6. Finkelstein, *Ox*, 7–47; Loewenstamm, *Studies*, 146–53.

not carry out the judgments of the great gods"), and the remedy for her defilement, she says, is marriage.[7]

From the Mari archives comes a decree by an anonymous prophet of Dagan: "Give orders to the cities to return the taboo material (*asakku*). Whoever commits an act of violence shall be expelled from the city" (*ARM* 26 206:17–22). From around 1400 BC comes the Hittite "Instructions for the Border Guards," where certain sexual offenders are banished, and the entire community must perform a self-purification ritual. From the same period at Ugarit comes a text where the king banishes conspirators for making counterfeit royal seals and documents (*Ras Shamra* 16:249, lines 13–19, 22, 25–26). From the late second millennium BC in Egypt comes nine examples of the standard oath taken in court: "If I speak falsehood, may I be mutilated and sent to Kush" (meaning Nubia).[8] In another case from Egypt, an adulterer is forbidden to ever see his lover again, on penalty of being sent to Kush (*Papyrus Deir el-Medina* 27). Egypt also gives us the Edict of Horemheb (involving banishment to the Sinai frontier), the Banishment Stela of Menkheperre (involving banishment to the El Kharga Oasis), and the Piankhi Prohibition Stela, where certain murderers are banned from the temple of Amun.[9] The *Chicago Assyrian Dictionary* (19:61) lists nineteen examples of exiled political figures, many of them from Old Babylonian omen texts, which seem to show that banishment was proverbial, although we are not sure if these are intended to be cases of banishment or fugitives.

From the first millennium BC comes a number of references to banishment by the Assyrians, including decrees that an offender will be forbidden to walk in temple or palace.[10] Similarly, during this same period in Israel, Abiathar is banished to Anathoth from his priesthood post by Solomon (1 Kgs 2:27), and Jeremiah is barred from entering the Jerusalem temple (Jer 36:5). In the post-exilic period, we have two clear references to banishment in Ezra (Ezra 7:26, an edict from Artaxerxes; and Ezra 10:8), another punitive expulsion by Nehemiah (Neh 13:28–29), the Maccabean-era reference in Josephus, the practice of expulsion at Qumran, as well as

---

7. Gurney, "Sultantepe Tablets," 122–23.

8. Peet, *Tomb-Robberies*, 146–53.

9. Schäfer, "Bannstela," *Urkunden* III, lines 110–13.

10. *RIMA* 3 A.O.104.9, rev., lines 10–14; ADD 647 = K 211, rev., line 29; NARGD 37, rev., lines 2–4; ABL 1105, rev., line 11–12; K 1033 = ABL 58, rev., line 9; ABL 505, lines 9–12; ABL 712, rev., lines 2–7.

the rabbinic practice of excommunication, where twenty-four offenses are said to call for this punishment by the Jerusalem Talmud. (Since the Talmud does not give a list, Strack and Billerbeck attempt to identify these offenses, using evidence from the Babylonian Talmud.)[11]

Three purposes of punitive expulsion reveal themselves in the above Near Eastern evidence. The first purpose is political, to deprive a person who is a political threat of the ability to participate in society. The second purpose is mercy, where expulsion is practiced as a less drastic punishment than death. The third purpose is removal of contamination to avoid the wrath of deity upon the community, a purpose that is particularly evident in both the Hittite case of *ḫurkel* and the Sumerian case of the *uzug*.

The Near Eastern evidence cited above establishes the plausibility of the expulsion penalty in Israel as a combination of mercy for a crime that deserves death, plus removal of contamination. The evidence demonstrates a clear precedent in the second millennium BC for such expulsion, and it documents the use of such expulsion in the ancient Near East throughout the biblical period. We also see clear evidence that such expulsion was practiced by post-exilic Jews, even though that practice is not clearly connected to the language of *kareth*.

CH §154 is the closest parallel to what is proposed to be biblical *kareth*: a provision in a legal code that punishes by geographic expulsion from one's city a perpetrator of a sex crime like the kinds described in Leviticus 18, a penalty more merciful than death, a penalty that also removes what was apparently viewed as a source of contamination. Similarly, we have the myth of Enlil and Ninlil, where a shocking sex crime is involved, and where expulsion rather than death is decreed by the gods. Hittite practice becomes the next closest parallel: expulsion is clearly practiced, by local option, as a merciful commutation of capital punishment in the standard legal code, and the motive to remove contamination is clearly in evidence.

Royal decrees become the next closest parallels to *kareth*. The closest parallel is the case from Ugarit, where the crime of counterfeiting a royal seal and royal documents parallels the counterfeiting of sacred oil and incense in Exodus 30, and in this case at Ugarit, a merciful alternative to death is provided. The next closest parallel is the decree by the prophet of Dagan at Mari, where the offense appears to be a cultic offense, but the punishment stops mercifully short of death.

11. Strack and Billerbeck, *Kommentar*, 4/1:309–13.

If *kareth* is indeed expulsion in codified form, its presence and its frequency in the Torah becomes unique among Near Eastern sources. Only Qumran, at the very end of the period in view, offers codified punitive expulsion on any comparable scale. Nevertheless, without the Near Eastern evidence, the argument that *kareth* was originally intended as punitive expulsion would be difficult to maintain based on logic and lexical evidence alone. But if *kareth* is a curse rather than a codified punishment, it becomes unusual among the curses of the Torah, which are practically never mixed together with statutes. This is possibly the strongest argument against Wold and Milgrom's theory: no ancient Near Eastern law code contains any divine extermination curse within its body of stipulations.

So how did an original practice of punitive expulsion ever get turned into a divine extermination curse? Here, we cannot prove, we can only theorize from the evidence. The shift seems to have happened in four stages. If one begins from the common observation that ʿ*am* in the plural appears to be an archaic term for extended family or relatives, then "cut off from one's people" (using the plural) appears to have originated in pre-Mosaic times as expulsion from one's clan. In the second stage, ʿ*am* either appears in the singular or is replaced by "congregation" or Israel, making it plain that "people" = the people of God as a whole, the nation. Here, punitive expulsion is still probable, but the language is more specific as to "cut off from where?" The shift to an extermination curse is evident by the time we get to Jeremiah and particularly Ezekiel, where the use of *karath* to mean "expulsion" has been forgotten and the use to mean "destruction" takes over. However, the precedent for the shift may be found in a few of the *kareth* texts themselves, where God is the subject and the verb is in the hipʿil conjugation. Finally, the Septuagint takes the "extermination" sense and makes it virtually the only way it translates *karath*, and Josephus, Philo, and the rabbis follow the same path.

A common question (for which, again, all we can do is theorize from the evidence) is how punitive expulsion would have been practiced. Qumran clearly kicks people out of their members-only town. They even give us the ceremony they used in 4Q266. Qumran also forbids any contact with the expelled person. In the post-exilic period, it is clear from all the examples we have that the expelled person was driven out of town. Evidence indicates that before the Exile, the focus for this penalty is on excluding the guilty party from the Temple. 2 Chronicles 23:19 tells that during the reign of Joash (mid-ninth century BC), Jehoiada the high priest "stationed the gatekeepers at the gates of the house of YHWH so that no one should enter who was in any way unclean." It is unclear how these gatekeepers were to determine the clean or unclean status of those who would enter the Temple; perhaps this involved the use of questioning under oath. Such a screening provision may explain how Jeremiah could be kept excluded from the Temple. Such gatekeepers were still employed for the same purpose late in the Second Temple period, according to Philo. The Mishnah (*m. Kel.* 1:8) states that no one with a discharge, no menstruant, and no woman who had just given birth was allowed to enter the Temple Mount. It would be up to gatekeepers to maintain the sanctity of the Temple Mount by keeping out the unclean and those who have been excommunicated. Like Qumran, the rabbis in the Talmud forbade contact with the expelled person.

Another common question is whether those who are "cut off" from God's people are lost. My ultra-short answer is, Look at the Babylonian exile. God's people were expelled from their land, but that doesn't mean they were cut off from God's saving love.

Taken together, the evidence shows that the penalty "cut off from one's people" in the Torah in most cases probably refers to a punitive removal from the community. While it is easy to trace the origins of the Wold-Milgrom divine-extermination theory back through the rabbinic sources to the Septuagint, a different interpretative tradition may be traced back from Qumran and the Samaritan community through the Maccabean period (as described by Josephus) to Ezra's fifth century community. It is my conclusion that it is the latter tradition of punitive expulsion that faithfully preserves the meaning of a penalty whose meaning had been lost to the greater part of Israel.

The conclusion of this study is that "cut off from one's people" is an expression of relative mercy, and it preserves the possibility of repentance. It also removes a source of ongoing moral contamination that puts the community at risk. "Cut off from one's people" is the equivalent of a life sentence in a prison without bars.

The conclusion that *kareth* is a form of punitive expulsion makes more sense out of the data than the theory that *kareth* is a divine extermination curse, for which there is no evidence as a penalty in the legal provisions of any ancient Near Eastern law code.

Appendix 2

Aselgeia: Jesus' Term for Homosexual Behavior?

Summary of an article *"Aselgeia* in Mark 7:22" by the author that appears in *Filologia Neotestamentaria* 21 (2008) 65–74

IN A POWERPOINT PRESENTATION that More Light Presbyterians produced to persuade the 2001 Presbyterian Church (USA) General Assembly to ordain practicing gays and lesbians, the narrator wraps up his presentation by saying, "We want to conclude this presentation by showing you what Jesus had to say about homosexuality." The next slide is a totally dark screen.

So Jesus never spoke one word about homosexuality? No. One can say that he actually spoke two. As we look at his sin list in Mark 7:21–23, we find two words that arguably include homosexual behavior within the scope of their meaning. One is the term *porneia* (sex outside of marriage), a word which has been much studied and commented upon. The other is the word *aselgeia*, a word on which precious little study has been done.

The great Bible commentator William Barclay considers *aselgeia* to be possibly the "ugliest word" in the list of New Testament sins. He capsulizes the word's meaning as "utter shamelessness."[1] It is variously translated as "licentiousness," "wantonness," and "lasciviousness." It's a word that Jesus (through Mark, his translator) might easily have enlisted as a euphemism or synonym for homosexual activity and other similarly shocking behavior forbidden by the Jewish law.

1. Barclay, *New Testament Words*, 60.

ANCIENT USES OF ASELGEIA

Aselgeia is mostly used to denote extremes of violence, sexual licentiousness, or insolence. Some specific examples from Plutarch help to narrow down what kind of behavior is intended when *aselgeia* is used to refer to sexual misdeeds. In *Parallela minora* 311.A.5, Smyrna falls in love with her father Cimyras and tricks him into consorting with her in the dark. When Cimyras finds out the truth, he pursues this "most wanton woman" (*tēn aselgestatēn*) with the sword. In *Parallela minora* 314.A.11, Phaedrea is described as "the wanton woman" (*hē aselgēs)* for falling in love with her step-son and pursuing him. In *Pelopidas* 28.5.1, Plutarch speaks of a woman oppressed by a tyrant who, "in addition to his other debaucheries (*aselgeias*), had made her youngest brother his paramour."

Demosthenes accuses a man of treating his slave-girl *aselgōs* by having sex with her openly at parties (*Neaer.* 59.33.1). Finally, a Cynic writer (Heraclitus, *Epistle 7*.5) complains of "a single young man who through licentiousness (*aselgeian*) is the lover of an entire city."[2]

Jewish writers almost always use this word in its sexual sense. In his comments on Galatians 5:20, J. B. Lightfoot writes, "A man may be *akathartos* [impure] and hide his sin; he does not become *aselgēs*, until he shocks public decency."[3] The term may have been used to refer to what were regarded as the most shameless violations of the sexuality taught in the Torah. For instance, in *Testament of Levi* 17:11, the Jewish writer lumps "licentious persons" directly together with "the lawless, pederasts, those who practice bestiality." Philo (*Spec.* 3:23) uses the word to describe the "lewdness" of marriage to one's own sister.

Josephus (*War* 4.562) speaks of a Zealot named Simon and his buddies who invade the Temple during the insanity of 68 AD and proceed to imitate the dress and passions of women, devising in their "extreme lasciviousness" (*hyperbolen aselgeian*) unlawful pleasures and wallowing as in a brothel. Josephus also tells (*Ant.* 20.112) of a Roman soldier on guard in the Temple portico during Passover who uncovers and exposes his genitals to the multitude; he laments the fact that 20,000 stampede and die that day because of the "indecent behavior (*aselgeia*) of one soldier."

---

2. In my original article, I overlooked a passage in Pseudo-Lucian (*Erōtēs* 28) where Charicles refers to lesbian "licentiousness" (*aselgeia*) and the use of "licentious instruments" (*aselga organa*) for them to simulate the male sexual organs.

3. Lightfoot, *Galatians*, 210–11.

NEW TESTAMENT USES OF ASELGEIA

Whatever it is, one can see why *aselgeia* appears on Jesus' sin list.

Aselgeia is used ten times in the New Testament. In Romans 13:13, Paul urges his readers to conduct themselves "not in promiscuity (*koitai*) or licentiousness (*aselgeia*)." Paul includes this term among the deeds of sinful human nature in Galatians 5:19, sandwiched in between illicit sex (*porneia*), impurity, idolatry, and witchcraft.

In 2 Corinthians 12:21, Paul laments those who "have not repented of the impurity, *porneia*, and *aselgeia* they have practiced." And in his description of the Gentiles in Ephesians 4:19, Paul says, "They have become callous and have given themselves up to *aselgeia*, greedy to practice every kind of uncleanness." Likewise, *aselgeia* tops the list of objectionable Gentile behaviors in 1 Peter 4:3, followed by "passions, drunkenness, revels, carousing, and lawless idolatry."

Second Peter uses *aselgeia* more than any other New Testament document. It links *aselgeia* explicitly with the sins of Sodom and Gomorrah, picturing Lot (2:7) as "greatly distressed by the licentiousness (*aselgeia*) of the wicked" around him (probably not referring to their failure to show hospitality). The author likens the men of Sodom to the false teachers of his day: "uttering loud boasts of folly, they entice with licentious passions (*aselgeiai*) people who have barely escaped from those who live in error" (2 Pet 2:18) And he warns that "many will follow their licentiousness, and because of them the way of truth will be reviled." (2 Pet 2:2)

EARLY CHRISTIAN USES OF ASELGEIA

In the patristic writers (such as Theophilus of Antioch, *Autol.* 3.3.12), *aselgeia* forms part of a standard trio of vices with *porneia* and *moicheia*, all three ostensibly sexual in nature. It arguably parallels Boswell's "triple prohibition": *ou porneuseis, ou moicheuseis, ou paidophthorēseis* ("thou shalt not fornicate, thou shalt not commit adultery, thou shalt not practice pederasty") found in Barnabas (19.4), the *Didache* (2.2), Clement of Alexandria (*Prot.* 10.108.5.2; *Paed.* 2.10.89.1.2), and Athanasius (*Synt.* 1.5.1–2).[4] Boswell notes that John of Damascus uses *arsenokoitias* (Paul's term for same-sex intercourse) as the third element in his trio of sexual vices in *Sacra parallela* 2.11.

---

4. Boswell, *Tolerance*, 103n42.

In his sermon *On the Passover*, Melito (160 AD) uses the triple combination of *aselgeia*, *porneia*, and *moicheia* (364). Then, producing an indisputable link between *aselgeia* and homosexual practice, Melito describes as *aselgestera* ("most licentious," 388) cases where "father cohabits with his child, and son and with his mother, and brother with sister, and male with male, and each man neighing after the wife of his neighbor" (389–94).

WHAT WORD MIGHT JESUS HAVE USED?

What Aramaic word could Jesus have used, that Mark would have translated into Greek as *aselgeia*? Our best guess could be made by consulting the Syriac version. The Syriac version of Mark 7:22 uses a noun that means "harlotry, licentiousness, immodesty, or lewdness". The word is used in the Syriac New Testament only here, and in Galatians 5:19 and 1 Peter 4:3 (in all three cases, it translates *aselgeia*). The root of the word indicates something that produces a terrible stench.

Both the Old Latin and the Vulgate translate *aselgeia* in Mark 7:22 with the term *impudicitia*. The *Oxford Latin Dictionary* says that *impudicitia*, especially in referring to males, is "often used of homosexual vice."[5] Suetonius, writing about Julius Caesar (*Jul.* 52.3), says, "Lest there be any doubt in anyone's mind that he was notorious indeed both for his *impudicitia* and his adulteries, the elder Curio called him in one of his speeches 'every woman's man and every man's woman.'" It is this sense of *impudicitia* that is arguably the meaning behind Mark's use of *aselgeia* in transmitting the words of Jesus in Mark 7:22.

SHAMELESS DISREGARD

Exactly what did Jesus mean by using a word for "utter shamelessness"? What did he consider too far "over the line"? It is likely that Jesus had in mind what his fellow Jews (like the author of 2 Peter) meant when they used the word: images of Sodom and Gomorrah, images of outrageous violation of the one-flesh union of man and woman. Jesus would likely have shared Jude's concern about those who "twist the grace of God into *aselgeia*" (Jude 4).

John P. Meier writes, "On *sexual* matters, Jesus and the Essenes tend in the same direction: stringent standards and prohibitions . . . In a

---

5. See also Williams, *Roman Homosexuality*, 172–73.

sense, one could call both Jesus and the Essenes extreme conservatives . . . apart from the two special cases of divorce and celibacy, where he diverged from mainstream Judaism, his views *were* those of mainstream Judaism. Hence there was no pressing need for him to issue or for the earliest Christian Jews to enshrine moral pronouncements about matters on which all Law-abiding Jews agreed. If almost all Jews agreed that acts of fornication and adultery were wrong, there was no reason for Jesus, who shared these views (see, e.g., Mark 7:21–22; Luke 16:18) to exegete the obvious."[6] If Jesus disagreed with Judaism about homosexuality, he was in the perfect position to correct our understanding on the issue.

Jesus says that both *porneia* and *aselgeia* come from the heart, along with murder, theft, adultery, greed, wickedness, deceit, envy, slander, pride, and foolishness (Mark 7:21–23). As the debate about sexuality continues in today's society, Jesus' word about shameless disregard for boundaries in the area of sexual behavior deserves further consideration.

6. Meier, *Marginal Jew*, 3: 502–503.

Appendix 3

English Translation
of Pseudo-Cyprian's De aleatoribus

THE FOLLOWING IS A rough translation of some portions of the earliest Christian sermon on gambling (early to mid-third century AD). It is the only translation available in English. The Latin text translated here is the one published by Adolf Harnack, "Der pseudocyprianische Tractat de aleatoribus," *Texte und Untersuchungen zur Geschichte der altchristlichen Literatur*, Band 5, Heft 1 (Leipzig: J. C. Hinrichs, 1888), 19–30.

(5) . . . For many are those temptations, which are of the first order: idolatry, immorality, theft, burglary, greed, fraud, drunkenness, impatience, adultery, murder, jealousy, treachery, false testimony, false talk, hatred, boastfulness, wrongdoing, error, and whatever similar acts are congruent to these. To them also the dice board belongs. Here the devil stands with the deadly poison of the serpent and an enticement to corruption, which, while operating sight unseen, works destruction by an all-crushing embrace. That is why I urge you, O faithful ones, to beware of the hand, which is already cleansed from human sin, which has been admitted into the Divine sacrifice and which receives its very dignity from God which extends to the salvation of all people, the same hand of the person who utters divine oracles to the praise of the Lord, the same hand which the sign of Christ protects inscribed in the front parts, the same hand that consumes the divine sacrament, all of that only in order to be implicated by the snares of the devil, from which that hand suffers deprivation! I speak of the hand of the dice-player, which wrecks and condemns itself, the hand that is addicted to a wanton preoccupation. It is the dice board which is the spear of the devil, and causes an incurable wound.

(6) The dice board, I say, where the devil is preeminent, submitting souls to capture; and when he has captured and triumphed over them, there is treachery, false testimony. It is at the dice board, I say, where there are the frenzy of a madman, perjury for sale, and serpent-like conversation. There—rabid friendships! There—hard, brutal atrocious deeds! There—discord among brothers! There—uproar and savage audacity and insane mind and animal-like impatience! The dice board, I say, is where enormous fortunes are lost, revealing contentions and thief-like demented mind. O cruel hand, and armed to its own peril, by which the paternal goods and wealth compiled with sweat by one's ancestors, brings it to ruin by an ignominious pursuit. O cruel hand, noxious and sleepless, night and day continually armed by its own instruments, which while sinning condemns itself, and after sinning does not quit! O depraved hand, by its own weapons headed to the Lord's destruction, which with the most sordid air ruins its entire fortune, yet with so much increase in household goods and exceedingly abundant wealth, now is destitute and a pauper! It is the dice-cube which the law hates, which disgraceful crime follows, where temptation is manifest and penalty is hidden. The game board is a snare, and there are evils and enemies to trip one up, the board which does not confer gain but consumes it totally. From here people next become paupers, from here they ruin their own wealth, from here already they are overwhelmed by the consumption of all items of their mutual funds, from here they throw away their parental inheritance without any protest in court. What kind of person is it, O faithful, that while no one pursues them, they pursue themselves for spite, and disperse their paternal inheritance with numerous multiform bone bits? And all the while these same dice-players celebrate nighttime vigils with women prostitutes under control of their host behind closed doors: armed against themselves, filled with the wretched spirit of the devil. And there also they commit a double crime: here the noise of the dice clatters, there sexual immorality silently takes place. Here without any dignity of self-respect, without any excuse, one thinks to yield one's own goods in a disastrous pursuit, there one drinks the deadly poison in secret . . .

(8) Whoever plays on the dice board, and is obligated not to be a wrongdoer, who should be aware by now of what has long been known by servants of God, that frenzy is evil and venomous and will forever be tortured by the judgments of God by rotating fire. Whoever plays on the

dice board, is first obligated to sacrifice to the host of the game, which is not allowed for Christians to do, says the Lord: "Whoever sacrifices to gods other than the Lord alone shall be eradicated." And again: "Do not wish to sacrifice to alien gods nor incite me with the works of your hands to utterly destroy you." "If you are a Christian, whoever you are, and you play at the dice-table, no sacrifice is allowed; you are a participant of this crime according to the law. And the Lord certainly opposes you and says, "Go out from her, my people, lest you participate in her sins." And again: "Depart, depart, go out from her, you who carry the vessels of the Lord, and the unclean thing you have not touched." Whoever is a Christian, and you play dice, in the first place you ought to know that you are not a Christian, but pagan is your name, and anything that pertains to the sacrifice of the Lord, you pour into a vacuum. For thus says the Lord: "Anyone who is unclean must not touch the holy sacrifice," and again, "Whoever eats the sacrificial meat, and his uncleanness is upon him, that soul shall perish from the people." If you are a dice-player, and you say you are a Christian, you say what you are not, because you are a participant of the world. You cannot have friendship with Christ when you are a friend of Christ's enemy.

(9) You can tell what sort of demented mind the faithful dice-players have, where they behave like madmen and swear falsely with most furious voices, and with blurred vision by the deprivation of the devil they inflict the gambler's hand against itself. They speak evil, they bewitch themselves, they dishonor their parents from whom they came by the confusion of their present circumstances. The noise of the dice sounds publicly. They hasten to the violent death of their inheritance by their own hands. Nor does the wretched person understand that he injures himself, to whatever extent one engages oneself with dice. And when the trapped person has already been conquered, he is animated sweetly by the devil backward to more noxious pursuits. O dangerous art of fanatics and wanton pursuit, which leaves a person not rich but naked and destitute! O butcher hand, O noxious hand, which does not stop after gain is gone, but plays onward after losing! The Christian who plays dice pollutes the hand that offers sacrifice to the devil, under the authority of the game's host. And for that reason the Lord speaks indignantly to him on this matter: "Do not wish," he says, "to extend your hands toward injustice, nor provoke me, or I will not allow you any longer to persist upon the earth." And again, "Keep your hands from injustice, and do

not do evil any longer." And the blessed apostle Paul similarly says, "See to it, my brothers, not to be conformed to this world and its pomp and attractions and pleasures, but restrain yourselves from all the injustices of the world."

(10) It is obvious that for that which is a crime against God there is no excuse, nor any indulgence, nor is pardon given for anyone. In the Gospel of the Lord it says, "If anyone," it says, "speaks blasphemy against a fellow human, he shall be forgiven, but if anyone sins against the Holy Spirit, he shall not be forgiven, neither in this world or in the world to come." And again through the prophet: "If a man sins a sin against a man, one can intercede with the Lord for him, but if anyone sins against the Lord, who can intercede for him?" And the blessed apostle, the procurator and vicar of Christ, the agent of care for the church, speaks and says, "You are a temple of God, and in you Christ dwells; if anyone violates the temple of God, God will destroy him." Also in the Gospel the Lord rejects and reproaches sinners, saying, "Withdraw from me, all who practice injustice; I do not know you." Also John the apostle says, "Every person who sins, is not from God, but from the devil; and you know consequently for this reason who shall become a child of God, in order that the children of the devil may perish." Any dice-player, if you are a Christian, you are an enemy to your inheritance and to what is yours. Whoever you are, desist from that wretched insanity of yours! Why do you let yourself fall so far by the devil into the cords of death? Why do you throw away your fortune and your abundance with the most sordid air? Why do you entangle yourself with the cords of the world, so that you will be judged with the world? Why do you lack your enmity toward the praise of popular favor, with which it is necessary that you should suffer punishment?

(11) Better to be not a dice-player, but a Christian! Spread your money on the table of the Lord, where Christ presides, the angels watch, and the martyrs are present. Divide your inheritance among paupers, which by savage pursuit you may be about to ruin anyway. Give your riches over to Christ as the winner, as a slave called away by your Lord, summoned by the pursuit of becoming like God! Copy the skill of the Lord, which does not perish but rather collects reward! Restrain your depraved headlong fall! Let your constant play be with the poor! Let your frequent employment be with widows. Part with your property and your preparations, all of them, toward the pursuit of the church! Deposit

your gold, silver and all your money in heavenly treasures! Your properties and mansions remove by just deeds to Paradise, so that your sins may be donated for you as alms, and apply yourself continually to good works. Do not play with dice, where play is harmful and an immortal crime, where there is thoughtless demented mind, where there is no truth, but a column of beggars. Cut off from there your hand, and turn from there your heart! Extract the enemy's blinder from your eyes, and purify your hand from the sacrifice of the devil! Throw away from you the morality of the thief! Be patient and Christian. Let you and your life be just and with forethought in your operations. Flee the pursuing devil! Flee the dice, the enemy of your works! Let your pursuit be wisdom, let the advice of the Gospels train you, raise pure hands to Christ, so that you may be able to claim the Lord. Put dice out of your mind! Amen.

Bibliography

Amundsen, Darrel. *Medicine, Society, and Faith in the Ancient and Medieval Worlds.* Baltimore: Johns Hopkins University Press, 1996.

Barclay, William. *New Testament Words.* London: SCM, 1964.

Boswell, John. *Christianity, Social Tolerance, and Homosexuality: Gay People in Western Europe from the Beginning of the Christian Era to the Fourteenth Century.* Chicago/London: University of Chicago Press, 1980.

Brunner, Theodore F. "Marijuana in Ancient Greece and Rome? The Literary Evidence." *Journal of Psychedelic Drugs* 9 (1977) 221–25.

Budziszewski, J. *What We Can't Not Know: A Guide.* Dallas: Spence, 2003.

Collins, Raymond F. *Sexual Ethics in the New Testament: Behavior and Belief.* New York: Crossroad Publishing, 2000.

Danby, Herbert. *The Mishnah: Translated from the Hebrew with Introduction and Brief Explanatory Notes.* Oxford: Oxford University Press, 1933.

Elliger, Karl. *Leviticus.* Handbuch zum Alten Testament 4. Tübingen: J. C. B. Mohr, 1966.

Epstein, Isidore, ed. *The Babylonian Talmud.* 18 vols. London: Soncino, 1978.

Fee, Gordon. *1 and 2 Timothy, Titus.* Good News Commentary. San Francisco: Harper & Row, 1984.

Finkelstein, Jacob J. *The Ox That Gored.* Transactions of the American Philosophical Society 71/2. Philadelphia: American Philosophical Society, 1981.

Gagnon, Robert A. J. *The Bible and Homosexual Practice: Texts and Hermeneutics.* Nashville: Abingdon, 2001.

Galen. *Claudii Galeni opera omnia.* Edited by Karl Gottleb Kühn, Friedrich Assmann, and Konrad Schubring. 20 vols. Hildesheim: G. Olms, 1986–2001.

Goldingay, John. *Theological Diversity and the Authority of the Old Testament.* Grand Rapids: Eerdmans, 1987.

Good, Edwin. "Capital Punishment and Its Alternatives in Ancient Near Eastern Law." *Stanford Law Review* 19 (1966–67) 947–77.

Gorman, Michael. *Abortion and the Early Church: Christian, Jewish, and Pagan Attitudes in the Greco-Roman World.* Downers Grove: Inter-Varsity, 1982.

Greenberg, Moshe. "Some Postulates of Biblical Criminal Law." In *Yehezkel Kaufmann Jubilee Volume,* edited by Menahem Haran, 5–28. Jerusalem: Magnes, 1960.

Gurney, Oliver R. "The Sultantepe Tablets (Continued): VII. The Myth of Nergal and Ereshkigal." *Anatolian Studies* 10 (1960) 105–31.

Harnack, Adolf. "Der pseudocyprianische Tractat de aleatoribus." In *Texte und Untersuchungen zur Geschichte der altchristlichen Literatur,* Band 5, Heft 1, 19–30. Leipzig: J. C. Hinrichs, 1888.

Harris, Lynn. "Casual Sex: Why Confident Women Are Saying No." *Glamour* 95/9 (1997) 314–15, 335–36.

Hobson, G. Thomas. "*Aselgeia* in Mark 7:22." *Filologia Neotestamentaria* 21 (2008) 65–74.

———. "Cut Off From (One's) People: Punitive Expulsion in the Torah." PhD diss., Concordia Seminary—St. Louis, 2010.

Hoffner, Harry A., Jr. "Symbols for Masculinity: Their Use in Ancient Near Eastern Sympathetic Magic Rituals." *Journal of Biblical Literature* 85 (1966) 326–34.

Krantz, Judith. "Living Together Is a Rotten Idea." *Cosmopolitan* 181/4 (October 1976) 218–27.

Lafont, Sophie. *Femmes, Droit, et Justice dans l'Antiquite orientale*. Orbis Biblicus et Orientalis 165. Fribourg: Editions Universitaires, 1999.

Levine, Baruch A. *Leviticus (ויקרא): The Traditional Hebrew Text with the New JPS Translation*. JPS Torah Commentary. Philadelphia: Jewish Publication Society, 1989.

Lightfoot, J. B. *Saint Paul's Epistle to the Galatians: A Revised Text With Introduction, Notes, and Dissertations*. London: Macmillan, 1890.

Loewenstamm, Samuel. *Comparative Studies in Biblical and Ancient Oriental Literatures*. Alter Orient und Altes Testament 204. Kevalaer: Neukirchener Verlag, 1980.

Martin, Dale. "It's About Sex . . . Not Homosexuality." Online: http://www.mlp.org/article.php/resourcepacket.

Meier, John P. *A Marginal Jew: Rethinking the Historical Jesus*. 4 vols. New York: Doubleday, 2001–.

Milgrom, Jacob. *Leviticus 1–16: A New Translation with Introduction and Commentary*. Anchor Bible 3. New York: Doubleday, 1991.

———. *Leviticus 17–22: A New Translation with Introduction and Commentary*. Anchor Bible 3A. New York: Doubleday, 2000.

Mooney, Alexander. "Evangelist accuses Obama of 'distorting' Bible." Online: http://www.cnn.com/2008/POLITICS/06/24/evangelical.vote/index.html.

Patrick, Dale. *Old Testament Law*. Atlanta: John Knox, 1985.

Paul, Shalom M. *Studies in the Book of the Covenant in Light of Cuneiform and Biblical Law*. Eugene, OR: Wipf and Stock, 2006.

Peet, Thomas Eric. *The Great Tomb-Robberies of the Twentieth Egyptian Dynasty*. Oxford: Clarendon, 1930; repr. Hildesheim/New York: Georg Olms, 1977.

Pope, Marvin. "Excommunication." In *IDB* 2:183–85.

Pseudo-Plutarch. *About Rivers and Mountains and Things Found in Them*. Translated by Thomas M. Banchich. Canisius College Translated Texts 4; Buffalo, N.Y.: Canisius College, 2010. Online: www.roman-emperors.org/Pseudo-P%20Revised.pdf.

Rad, Gerhard von. *Old Testament Theology*. Translated by D. M. G. Stalker. 2 vols. New York: Harper, 1962.

Schäfer, Heinrich, ed. "Bannstela." In *Urkunden* III, *Urkunden der Älteren Athiopenkönige*, 110–13. Leipzig: J. C. Hinrichs, 1905.

Schwartz, David G. *Roll the Bones: the History of Gambling*. New York: Gotham Books, 2006.

Scott, Samuel Parsons. *The Civil Law: including the Twelve Tables, the Institutes of Gaius, the Rules of Ulpian, the Opinions of Paulus, the Enactments of Justinian, and the Constitutions of Leo*. New York: AMS Press, 1973.

Steinmetz, Andrew. *The Gaming Table: its votaries and victims, in all times and countries, especially in England and in France*. 2 vols. Montclair, N.J.: Patterson Smith, 1969.

Strack, Hermann, and Paul Billerbeck. *Kommentar zum Neuen Testament aus Talmud und Midrasch.* 5 vols. Munich: C. H. Beck, 1956.

Tacitus, Cornelius. "A Treatise on the Situation, Manners, and Inhabitants of Germany," n. p. Online:http://www.elfinspell.com/TacitusGermany3.html#refch24.

Thompson, R. Campbell. *Dictionary of Assyrian Botany.* London: British Academy, 1949.

Westbrook, Raymond. *Studies in Biblical and Cuneiform Law.* Paris: Gabalda, 1988.

Westermann, Claus. *Genesis 12–36: A Commentary.* Translated by John J. Scullion. Minneapolis: Augsburg, 1985.

Williams, Craig A. *Roman Homosexuality: Ideologies of Masculinity in Classical Antiquity.* New York/Oxford: Oxford University Press, 1999.

Wold, Donald. "The Meaning of the Biblical Penalty 'Kareth.'" PhD diss., University of California at Berkeley, 1978.

Zimmerli, Walther. "Die Eigenart der prophetischen Rede des Ezechiel." *Zeitschrift für die alttestamentiche Wissenschaft* 66 (1954) 1–26.